The Right Decision Every Time

Published by
Lotus Press

The Right Decision Every Time

Dr. Aditya Sachdev

Lotus
PRESS

4263/3, Ansari Road,
Darya Ganj, New Delhi-110002

LOTUS PRESS
4263/3, Ansari Road, Darya Ganj, New Delhi-110002
Ph: 32903912, 23280047, E-mail: lotus_press@sify.com

The Right Decision Every Time

ISBN 81-2382-168-5

Published by: Lotus Press, New Delhi-110002
Laser type set by: Reliable Infomedia, New Delhi-110009
Printed at: Nisha Enterprises, Delhi.

PREFACE

If shorn of the glamorous trappings that come with the high profile job, the corporate executive of today can really be seen for who he/she is: a most stressed individual constantly in conflict with various elements in an unforgiving, highly competitive environment. Executives of the modern workplace are usually confronted with challenges that exact the best of their decision-making abilities: a task easier to say so than perform, riddled as each decision, is with numerous implications and consequences. In such a scenario, making the right decision seems nothing less than an arduous, Herculean task, calling for every ounce of managerial skills to be used and handled in a deft manner.

This book realising the need for managers and executives for a survival guide on decision-making in the corporate world, has been conceptualised and written as a self-help manual. Guiding readers through the refuddling maze of decisions and their results, it enables them to grasp the fundamentals of the right thinking process which can immeasurably clarify the ways of making decision for numerous situations. Comprehending the changing nature of the dynamic arena that is the corporate world, the book generally caters to all executives, but specifically to those in senior managerial positions, as they are the ones who usually face dilemmas which are in need of tough decisions. With situational examples, seasoned and experienced advice on corporate matters, it helps readers take a responsible stance on their difficult decisions, and execute them unwaveringly. Lucid, comprehensive and insightful, and incorporating germs of advice on the corporate decision-making process, it is hoped that the book proves resourceful for the readers.

Editor

CONTENTS

1

IMPORTANCE OF DECISION-MAKING

DEFINITION

Decision-making is the study of identifying and choosing alternatives based on the values and preferences of the decision-maker. Making a decision implies that there are alternative choices to be considered, and in such a case we want not only to identify as many of these alternatives as possible but to choose the one that best fits with our goals, desires, lifestyle, values, and so on.

Decision-making is also defined as the process of sufficiently reducing uncertainty and doubt about alternatives to allow a reasonable choice to be made from among them. This definition stresses the information gathering function of decision-making. It should be noted here that uncertainty is *reduced* rather than eliminated. Very few decisions are made with absolute certainty because complete knowledge about all the alternatives is seldom possible. Thus, every decision involves a certain amount of risk.

TYPES OF DECISIONS

There are several basic kinds of decisions.

1. *Decisions whether.* This is the yes/no, either/or

decision that must be made before we proceed with the selection of an alternative. Should I buy a new Car? Should I travel this summer? Decisions whether are made by weighing reasons pro and con. It is important to be aware of having made a decision whether, since too often we assume that decision-making begins with the identification of alternatives, *assuming that the decision to choose one has already been made.*

2. *Decisions which.* These decisions involve a choice of one or more alternatives from among a set of possibilities, the choice being based on how well each alternative measures up to a set of predefined criteria.
3. *Contingent decisions.* These are decisions that have been made but put on hold until some condition is met.

Most people carry around a set of already made, contingent decisions, just waiting for the right conditions or opportunity to arise. Time, energy, price, availability, opportunity, encouragement—all these factors can figure into the necessary conditions that need to be met before we can act on our decision.

COMPONENTS OF DECISION-MAKING

Decision Environment

Every decision is made within a decision environment, which is defined as the collection of information, alternatives, values, and preferences *available at the time of the decision.* An ideal decision environment would include all possible information, all of it accurate, and every possible alternative. However, both information and alternatives are constrained because time and effort to gain information or identify alternatives are limited. The time constraint simply means that a decision must be made by a certain time.

The effort constraint reflects the limits of manpower, money, and priorities. Since decisions must be made within this constrained environment, we can say that *the major challenge of decision-making is uncertainty,* and a major goal of decision analysis is to reduce uncertainty. We can almost never have all information needed to make a decision with certainty, so most decisions involve an undeniable amount of risk.

The fact that decisions must be made within a limiting decision environment suggests two things. First, it explains why hindsight is so much more accurate and better at making decisions that foresight. As time passes, the decision environment continues to grow and expand. New information and new alternatives appear—even after the decision must be made. Armed with new information after the fact, the hindsighters can many times look back and make a much better decision than the original maker, *because the decision environment has continued to expand.*

The second thing suggested by the decision-within-an-environment idea follows from the above point. Since the decision environment continues to expand as time passes, it is often advisable to put off making a decision until close to the deadline. Information and alternatives continue to grow as time passes, so to have access to the most information and to the best alternatives, do not make the decision too soon. Now, since we are dealing with real life, it is obvious that some alternatives might no longer be available if too much time passes; that is a tension we have to work with, a tension that helps to shape the cutoff date for the decision.

Delaying a decision as long as reasonably possible, then, provides three benefits:

1. The decision environment will be larger, providing more information. There is also time for more thoughtful and extended analysis.
2. New alternatives might be recognised or created.
3. The decision-maker's preferences might change. With further thought, wisdom, maturity, you may decide not to buy car X and instead to buy car Y.

Effects of Quantity on Decision-Making

Many decision-makers have a tendency to seek more information than required to make a good decision. When too much information is sought and obtained, one or more of several problems can arise.

1. A delay in the decision occurs because of the time required to obtain and process the extra information. This delay could impair the effectiveness of the decision or solution.
2. Information overload will occur. In this state, so much information is available that decision-making ability actually declines because the information in its entirety can no longer be managed or assessed appropriately. A major problem caused by information overload is forgetfulness. When too much information is taken into memory, especially in a short period of time, some of the information will be pushed out.
3. Selective use of the information will occur. That is, the decision-maker will choose from among all the information available only those facts which support a preconceived solution or position.
4. Mental fatigue occurs, which results in slower work or poor quality work.
5. Decision fatigue occurs, where the decision-maker tires of making decisions. Often the result is fast,

careless decisions or even decision paralysis—no decisions are made at all.

The quantity of information that can be processed by the human mind is limited. Unless information is consciously selected, processing will be biased toward the first part of the information received. After that, the mind tires and begins to ignore subsequent information or forget earlier information.

Nature of Decision Streams

A common misconception about decision-making is that decisions are made in isolation from each other: you gather information, explore alternatives, and make a choice, without regard to anything that has gone before. The fact is, decisions are made in a context of other decisions. The typical metaphor used to explain this is that of a stream. There is a stream of decisions surrounding a given decision, many decisions made earlier have led up to this decision and made it both possible and limited. Many other decisions will follow from it.

Another way to describe this situation is to say that most decisions involve a choice from a group of preselected alternatives, made available to us from the universe of alternatives by the previous decisions we have made. Previous decisions have "activated" or "made operable" certain alternatives and "deactivated" or "made inoperable" others.

We might say, then, that every decision

1. follows from previous decisions,
2. enables many future decisions, and
3. prevents other future decisions.

People who have trouble making decisions are sometimes trapped by the constraining nature of decision-making.

Every decision you make precludes other decisions, and therefore might be said to cause a loss of freedom. If you decide to marry Terry, you no longer can decide to marry Shawn. However, just as making a decision causes a loss of freedom, it also creates new freedom, new choices and new possibilities. So making a decision is liberating as well as constraining. And a decision left unmade will often result in a decision by default or a decision being made for you. It is important to realise that every decision you make affects the decision stream and the collections of alternatives available to you both immediately and in the future. In other words, decisions have far reaching consequences.

Concepts of Decision-Making

1. *Information.* This is knowledge about the decision, the effects of its alternatives, the probability of each alternative, and so forth. A major point to make here is that while substantial information is desirable, the statement that "the more information, the better" is not true. Too much information can actually reduce the quality of a decision.
2. *Alternatives.* These are the possibilities one has to choose from. Alternatives can be identified or even developed. Merely searching for preexisting alternatives will result in less effective decision-making.
3. *Criteria.* These are the characteristics or requirements that each alternative must possess to a greater or lesser extent. Usually the alternatives are rated on how well they possess each criterion.
4. *Goals.* What is it you want to accomplish? Strangely enough, many decision-makers collect a bunch of alternatives and then ask, "Which should I choose?" without thinking first of what their goals

are, what overall objective they want to achieve. Next time you find yourself asking, "What should I do? What should I choose?" ask yourself first, "What are my goals?" A component of goal identification should be included in every instance of decision analysis.

5. *Value.* Value refers to how desirable a particular outcome is, the value of the alternative, whether in rupees, satisfaction, or other benefit.

6. *Preferences.* These reflect the philosophy and moral hierarchy of the decision-maker. We could say that they are the decision-maker's "values," but that might be confusing with the other use of the word, above. If we could use that word here, we would say that personal values dictate preferences. Some people prefer excitement to calmness, certainty to risk, efficiency to esthetics, quality to quantity, and so on. Thus, when one person chooses to ride the wildest roller coaster in the park and another chooses a mild ride, both may be making good decisions, if based on their individual preferences.

7. *Decision Quality.* This is a rating of whether a decision is good or bad. A good decision is a logical one based on the available information and reflecting the preferences of the decision-maker.

   The important concept to grasp here is that the quality of a decision is not related to its outcome: a good decision can have either a good or a bad outcome. Similarly, a bad decision can still have a good outcome. Good decisions that result in bad outcomes should thus not be cause for guilt or recrimination. If you decide to take the scenic route based on what you know of the road and your preferences, then your decision is a good one, even though you might happen to get in an accident, or have a flat tire in the middle of nowhere. It is not justified to say, "Well, this was a bad decision."

In judging the quality of a decision, in addition to the concerns of logic, use of information and alternatives, three other considerations come into play:

(*a*) The decision must meet the stated objectives most thoroughly and completely. How well does the alternative chosen meet the goals identified?

(*b*) The decision must meet the stated objectives most efficiently, with concern over cost, energy, side effects. Are there negative consequences to the alternative that make that choice less desirable? We sometimes overlook this consideration in our search for thrills.

(*c*) The decision must take into account valuable byproducts or indirect advantages. A new employee candidate may also have extra abilities not directly related to the job but valuable to the company nonetheless. These should be taken into account.

8. *Acceptance.* Those who must implement the decision or who will be affected by it must accept it both intellectually and emotionally. Acceptance is a critical factor because it occasionally conflicts with one of the quality criteria. In such cases, the best thing to do may be to choose a lesser quality solution that has greater acceptance.

Thus, the inferior method may produce greater results if the inferior one has greater support. One of the most important considerations in decision-making, then, is the people factor. Always consider a decision in light of the people implementation.

A decision that may be technologically brilliant but that is sociologically stupid will not work. Only decisions that are implemented, and implemented with thoroughness will work the way they are intended to.

Major Approaches to Decision-Making

There are two major approaches to decision-making in-an organisation, the authoritarian method in which an executive figure makes a decision for the group and the group method in which the group decides what to do.

1. *Authoritarian.* The manager makes the decision based on the knowledge he can gather. He then must explain the decision to the group and gain their acceptance of it. In some studies, the time breakdown for a typical operating decision is something like this: make decision, 5 min.; explain decision, 30 min.; gain acceptance, 30 min.
2. *Group.* The group shares ideas and analyses, and agrees upon a decision to implement. Studies show that the group often has values, feelings, and reactions quite different from those the manager supposes they have. No one knows the group and its tastes and preferences as well as the group itself. And, interestingly, the time breakdown is something like this: group makes decision, 30 min.; explain decision, 0 min.; gain acceptance, 0 min.

Clearly, just from an efficiency standpoint, group decision-making is better. More than this, it has been shown many times that *people prefer to implement the ideas they themselves think of.* They will work harder and more energetically to implement their own idea than they would to implement an idea imposed on them by others. We all have a love for our own ideas and solutions, and we will always work harder on a solution supported by our own vision and our own ego than we will on a solution we have little creative involvement with.

There are two types of group decision-making sessions. First is free discussion in which the problem is simply put on the table for the group to talk about. The other kind of group decision-making is developmental discussion or structured discussion. Here the problem is broken down into steps, smaller parts with specific goals.

Decision-Making Strategies

As you know, there are often many solutions to a given problem, and the decision-maker's task is to choose one of them. The task of choosing can be as simple or as complex as the importance of the decision warrants, and the number and quality of alternatives can also be adjusted according to importance, time, resources and so on. There are several strategies used for choosing. Among them are the following:

1. *Optimising.* This is the strategy of choosing the best possible solution to the problem, discovering as many alternatives as possible and choosing the very best. How thoroughly optimising can be done is dependent on:
   - (*a*) Importance of the problem.
   - (*b*) Time available for solving it.
   - (*c*) Cost involved with alternative solutions.
   - (*d*) Availability of resources, knowledge.
   - (*e*) Personal psychology, values.
2. *Satisficing.* In this strategy, the first satisfactory alternative is chosen rather than the best alternative. If you are very hungry, you might choose to stop at the first decent looking restaurant in the next town rather than attempting to choose

the best restaurant from among all. The word *satisficing* was coined by combining *satisfactory* and *sufficient*. For many small decisions, such as where to park, what to drink, which pen to use, which tie to wear, and so on, the satisficing strategy is perfect.

3. *Maximax.* This stands for "maximise the maximums." This strategy focuses on evaluating and then choosing the alternatives based on their maximum possible payoff. This is sometimes described as the strategy of the optimist, because favourable outcomes and high potentials are the areas of concern. It is a good strategy for use when risk taking is most acceptable, when the go-for-broke philosophy is reigning freely.
4. *Maximin.* This stands for "maximise the minimums." In this strategy, that of the pessimist, the worst possible outcome of each decision is considered and the decision with the highest minimum is chosen. The Maximin orientation is good when the consequences of a failed decision are particularly harmful or undesirable. Maximin concentrates on the salvage value of a decision, or of the guaranteed return of the decision. It's the philosophy behind the saying, "A bird in the hand is worth two in the bush."

Quiz shows exploit the uncertainty many people feel when they are not quite sure whether to go with a maximax strategy or a maximin one: "Okay, Mrs. Saxena, you can now choose to take what you've already won and go home, or risk losing it all and find out what's behind door number three."

Procedure of Decision-Making

As you read this procedure, remember our discussion

earlier about the recursive nature of decision-making. In a typical decision-making situation, as you move from step to step here, you will probably find yourself moving back and forth also.

1. *Identify the decision to be made together with the goals it should achieve.* Determine the scope and limitations of the decision. Is the new job to be permanent or temporary or is that not yet known? Is the new package for the product to be put into all markets or just into a test market? How might the scope of the decision be changed—that is, what are its possible parameters?

   When thinking about the decision, be sure to include a clarification of goals: We must decide whom to hire for our new secretary, one who will be able to create an efficient and organised office. Or, We must decide where to go on vacation, where we can relax and get some rest from the fast pace of society.

2. *Get the facts.* But remember that you cannot get all the facts. Get as many facts as possible about a decision *within the limits of time imposed on you and your ability to process them,* but remember that virtually every decision must be made in partial ignorance. Lack of complete information must not be allowed to paralyse your decision. A decision based on partial knowledge is usually better than not making the decision when a decision is really needed. The proverb that "any decision is better than no decision," while perhaps extreme, shows the importance of choosing. When you are racing toward a bridge support, you must decide to turn away to the right or to the left. Which way you turn is less important than the fact that you do indeed turn.

As part of your collection of facts, list your feelings, hunches, and intuitive urges. Many decisions must ultimately rely on or be influenced by intuition because of the remaining degree of uncertainty involved in the situation.

Also as part of your collection of facts, consult those who will be affected by and who will have to implement your decision. Input from these people not only helps supply you with information and help in making the decision but it begins to produce the acceptance necessary in the implementers because they feel that they are part of the decision-making process. As Russell Ackoff noted in *The Art of Problem Solving*, not consulting people involved in a decision is often perceived as an act of aggression.

3. *Develop alternatives.* Make a list of all the possible choices you have, including the choice of doing nothing. Not choosing one of the candidates or one of the building sites is in itself a decision. Often a non decision is harmful as we mentioned above—not choosing to turn either right or left is to choose to drive into the bridge. But sometimes the decision to do nothing is useful or at least better than the alternatives, so it should always be consciously included in the decision-making process. Also be sure to think about not just identifying available alternatives but creating alternatives that don't yet exist.

4. *Rate each alternative.* This is the evaluation of the value of each alternative. Consider the negative of each alternative and the positive of each (money saved, time saved, added creativity or happiness to company or employees, etc.). Remember here that the alternative that you might like best or that would in the best of all possible worlds be an

obvious choice will, however, not be functional in the real world because of too much cost, time, or lack of acceptance by others.

Also don't forget to include indirect factors in the rating. If you are deciding between machines X, Y, and Z and you already have an employee who knows how to operate machine Z, that fact should be considered. If you are choosing an investigative team to send to Japan to look at plant sites and you have very qualified candidates A, B, and C, the fact that B is a very fast typist, a superior photographer or has some other side benefit in addition to being a qualified team member, should be considered. In fact, what you put on your hobbies and interests line on your resume can be quite important when you apply for a job just because employers are interested in getting people with a good collection of additional abilities.

5. *Rate the risk of each alternative.* In problem solving, you hunt around for a solution that best solves a particular problem, and by such a hunt you are pretty sure that the solution will work. In decision-making, however, there is always some degree of uncertainty in any choice. Will Aditya really work out as the new supervisor? If we decide to expand into Canada, will our sales and profits really increase? If we let Jimmy at age fifteen, will the experience be good? If you decide to marry person X or buy car Y or go to school Z, will that be the best or at least a successful choice?

   Risks can be rated as percentages, ratios, rankings, grades or in any other form that allows them to be compared.

6. *Make the decision.* If you are making an individual decision, apply your preferences. Choose the path

to follow, whether it includes one of the alternatives, more than one of them or the decision to choose none.

And of course, don't forget to implement the decision and then evaluate the implementation, just as you would in a problem solving experience. One important item often overlooked in implementation is that when explaining the decision to those involved in carrying it out or those who will be affected by it, don't just list the projected benefits: frankly explain the risks and the drawbacks involved and tell why you believe the proposed benefits outweigh the negatives. Implementers are much more willing to support decisions when they (1) understand the risks and (2) believe that they are being treated with honesty and like adults.

Remember also that very few decisions are irrevocable. Don't cancel a decision prematurely because many new plans require time to work—it may take years for your new branch office in Paris to get profitable—but don't hesitate to change directions if a particular decision clearly is not working out or is being somehow harmful. You can always make another decision to do something else.

DEGREE OF RISKING

Risk and uncertainty create anxiety, yet they are necessary components of an active life.

General Comments

1. *Only the risk takers are truly free.* All decisions of consequence involve risk. Without taking risks, you cannot grow or improve or even live.
2. *There is really no such thing as permanent security in anything on earth.* Not taking risks is really not more

secure than taking them, for your present state can always be changed without action on your part. If you don't take the risk of dying by driving to the store, your house could collapse on you and kill you anyway.

3. *You are supposed to be afraid when you risk.* Admit your fears—of loss, of rejection, of failure.
4. *Risking normally involves a degree of separation anxiety—the anxiety you feel whenever you are removed from something that makes you feel secure.* Many children feel this when they first leave their parents for school. Some college students feel this when they go off to college. Travellers sometimes feel it when they get homesick. The way to overcome separation anxiety is to build a bridge between the familiar and secure and the new. Find out what the new place—school or country—is like and how its elements compare to familiar and secure things at home. Take familiar things with you—books, teddy bear, popcorn popper, whatever.

The same is true of all risks. Make the opportunity as familiar as possible and learn as much about it as you can before you release the security of the old. Find out about the new job, its location, the lifestyle of those who live there, and so on.

Risk Evaluation Theory

The traditional strategy for evaluating risks is to use an expected value calculation, based on the simple idea that the expected value of a risk is the value of the possible outcome discounted by the probability of its realisation. The formula is EV=PR or expected value equals prize times risk. Thus, if you have one chance in a million of winning a million rupees, your expected value is one rupee. Expected value calculations are often used when comparing an amount of money to be invested with the probable payoff.

Let's take a typical state lottery, for example. The investment for a ticket is a 50 rupees. The usual prize is about one crore and the chance of winning is about one in 14,800,000. By discounting the possible outcome by the chance of winning, we discover that the expected value of the lottery ticket is about 43.9 paise. Since a ticket costs one rupee, we would conclude that this is a poor risk. Only when the expected value meets or exceeds the required expense is the risk considered worth taking, according to this theory.

Advices

1. *Decide whether the risk is necessary or desirable.* Spend some careful thought before acting, so that you will not end up taking unnecessary risks.
2. *Risk for the right reasons and when you are calm and thoughtful.* Don't take a risk because you are angry, hurt, depressed, desperate, or frightened. Don't take risks just to get revenge or to harm someone else. Don't risk when you are incapable of rational thought.
3. *Have a goal.* When you take a risk, have a clear purpose in mind so that you will know, after the fact, whether you succeeded or not. What will taking the risk accomplish?
4. *Determine the possible loss as well as the gain.* That is, know exactly what the consequences of failure will be. Unless you know pretty accurately what both loss and gain will be, you do not understand the risk. There is a tendency either to underestimate or to overestimate the consequences of risk. Underestimation can result in surprising damage, cost, setbacks, pain, whatever. But overestimation is

just as problematic, because it can keep us from taking the risks we should be taking. Many times, upon reflection, the worst case event of a failed risk is much less harmful or negative that we originally believed.

It's a good idea in fact to list all the good expected effects of a successful outcome and all the bad expected effects of an unsuccessful outcome.

5. *Try to make an accurate estimate about the probability of each case.* Is the probability of success one in two, one in ten, one in a hundred, one in a million? This can be sometimes difficult to do, but usually you can guess the probability within an order of magnitude.
6. *When possible, take one risk at a time.* Divide your actions or goals wherever possible so that you are not combining risks unless absolutely necessary. Simultaneous risking increases anxiety, creates confusion, and makes failure analysis very difficult.
7. *Use imaging or role playing to work through the various possibilities, successes and failures, so that you will be mentally prepared for any outcome.* Think about what can go right and what can go wrong and how you will respond to or adjust to each possibility.
8. *Use a plan.* Set up a timetable with a list of steps to take. Use the plan as a guideline, but be flexible.
9. *Act decisively.* When you have evaluated the risk and decided that it's worth it, act. Go for it. Don't hesitate at the threshold or halfway through. Once you get going, be courageous. Grit your teeth and move forward. Don't procrastinate and don't act half heartedly.
10. *Don't expect complete success.* You may get it, of course, but chances are the result of your risk will not be exactly what you had imagined and there

will be more a degree of success than absolute success or failure.

Strategies of Risk Management

In order of precedence, the strategies are:

1. *Dismiss extremely remote or unrealistic possibilities.* There are risks like dying on the freeway, being shot by robbers, buying poisoned food, and so forth, but these should not normally enter into the risk evaluation because they are highly if not extremely improbable. Remember that all life is accompanied by risk. Ten thousand television sets catch fire each year, a hundred thousand people walk through plate glass each year, 125,000 do-it-yourselfers injure themselves with power tools each year, 70,000 children are injured by toys each year, ten thousand people are poisoned by aspirin each year. But what are we willing to give up? Some of these are not really remote, but we are willing to take the risk. E.g. automobile deaths. 1 chance in 4000 each year of dying.

   And of course whenever you trust someone, you risk betrayal; when you open yourself, you risk exploitation or ridicule; whenever you hand over a dollar, you risk being defrauded.

2. *Insofar as possible, avoid catastrophes.* If there is a small but significant chance for catastrophe, then the regular expected value calculations may not apply.

   A major principle of risk management is to avoid any real risk of catastrophe at any reasonable cost. The difficulty of applying this principle comes from the uncertainty of what is a real risk and what is a reasonable cost.

3. *Recognise the tradeoffs.* Remember that every action of life has some risk to it. Even when we don't take the risk upon ourselves, risk is often put upon us by the nature of life and society. Eating you risk food poisoning or choking, but you have to eat or you'll die. Socialising you risk disease, driving or flying you risk crashing, but in some sense you have to socialise and travel. Lying in the sun you risk skin cancer; smoking you risk lung cancer; eating French fries you risk heart disease.
4. *Maximise Expected Values.* Normally, the expected value of each alternative shows its relative preferability. That is, you are opting for the greatest probability of the greatest good. Remember, though, that these calculations are guides, and are based on what may be very subjective probabilities and rewards. You are not "required by law" to choose any particular alternative. If you believe that the alternative with the highest EV is a poor choice, you should reconsider the probabilities and rewards you have assigned to all the alternatives.

With these ideas in mind, you'll better understand why some people pursue dangerous sports like skiing, sky diving, race car driving and so forth. The risk/benefit ratio is acceptable to them. It may be useful to note here, too, that most people are not rational risk takers. They take some risks all out of proportion to any expected return and avoid other risks that have a large expected value compared to the risk.

2

HOW TO MAKE GOOD DECISIONS

Good decision-making brings about a better life. It gives you some control over your life. In fact, many frustrations with oneself are caused by not being able to use one's own mind to understand the decision problem, and the courage to act upon it.

COMPONENTS OF DECISION-MAKING

There are four components of decision-making: data gathering, information processing, meaningmaking, and decision-making, or deciding on a course of action. We use our five senses to gather data from the outside world—*data gathering*. We use our brain to integrate the data from the five senses into information packages—*information processing*. The mind then compares the incoming information package with the information packages stored in memory to find a match—*meaning-making*.

When it finds a match, it releases the instructions attached to the memory along with any emotional charge associated with the memory, and these instructions result in actions and behaviours—*decision-making*. If the mind does not find a match, it uses reason and logic to formulate a response to the situation that is in alignment with its motivations.

The response will be determined by many factors, the most important of which will be the level of consciousness the mind is operating from—what is important to the individual at that moment in time. The instructions that are attached to memory are learned from previous experiences. The most deeply engrained instructions are those that we learned during childhood when our brain and mind were still growing and learning to cope with the world. The purpose of the instructions associated with a memory is to maintain or enhance internal stability and external equilibrium: the instructions tell us how to survive, how to feel safe and secure, and how to safeguard our self-respect.

Five Modes of Decision-Making

There are five modes of decision-making. The difference between each mode of decision-making is the amount of emphasis that is given to each of the four components of decision-making. The five modes of decision-making are based on instincts, subconscious beliefs, conscious beliefs, values, and intuition.

Instinct-based decision-making

Instinct-based decision-making is cellular based (DNA) and principally associated with issues of survival. For example, babies instinctively know how to suckle, how to cry when their needs are not being met, and how to smile so they get attention. No one taught them how to do this. It is encoded in the species DNA. In adult life, instinct-based decision-making kicks in to help us survive and avoid dangerous situations. In certain situations, our instincts may cause us to put our life at risk in order to the save the life of another.

The main features of *instinct-based decision-making* are:

1. Actions always precede thought—there is no pause between meaning-making and decision-making for reflection.
2. The decisions that are made are always based on past experiences—what our *species history* has taught us about how to survive and keep safe. These instructions are encoded in the cellular.
3. We are not in control of our actions and behaviours. They are in control of us.

Subconscious belief-based decision-making

In subconscious belief-based decision-making, we also react to what is happening in our world without reflection but on the basis of personal memories rather than cellular (DNA) memories. In this mode of decision-making action precedes thought. The action is often accompanied by the release of an emotional charge.

The emotional charge that accompanies the actions and behaviours in subconscious belief based decision-making can be positive or negative. Negatively charged emotions lead to the display of potentially limiting behaviours—blame, internal competition, rivalry, caution, etc. Positively charged emotions lead to the display of life-enhancing behaviours—openness, trust, cooperation, honesty, etc.

We know we are operating in this mode when we get angry, upset, shout at people, or generally behave badly towards others or in a self-serving manner. What is driving this behaviour is our subconscious fear-based beliefs around not having enough, not feeling safe or loved, not being enough, or not being respected—the fear-based beliefs associated with the first three levels of consciousness. These types of behaviour are always accompanied by a pent up negative emotional charge. We also display sub-conscious belief-based decision-making when we display positive emotions such as tears of joy and feelings of pride and spontaneous happiness.

In such cases, we are connecting with and releasing instructions associated with positively charged personal memories. Again, actions precede thought. Sub-conscious belief-based decision-making is similar to instinct-based decisionmaking. The only difference is that the memories and instructions that we are connecting with are contained in our personal memory, not in our cellular.

The main features of subconscious belief-based decision-making are:

1. Actions always precede thought—there is no gap between meaning-making and decision-making for reflection;
2. The decisions that are made are always based on past experiences—what our *personal history* has taught us about how to maintain or enhance internal stability and external equilibrium at an individual level. This history is stored in our personal memory;
3. We are not in control of our actions and behaviours. In this mode of decision-making the only way we can get back into conscious control is either to release or bottle-up our emotions. Releasing helps us to return to rationality. Bottling-up creates stress and frustration: we are storing up negative emotional energy for future release;
4. It is very personal. Others cannot be consulted to enhance meaning-making and give support in reaching a decision; and,
5. We are always operating from the shadow side of the first three levels of consciousness—the behaviours we are displaying are based on deeply held beliefs about not being able to survive with what we have (not having enough), not feeling safe

(not belonging), and/or not being respected (not being enough).

Conscious belief-based decision-making

If we want to make rational decisions, we have to leave behind subconscious belief-based decisionmaking and shift to conscious belief-based decision-making. We are able to make rational decisions because we insert a pause between meaning-making and decision-making.

The pause allows us time for reflection and thought so we can use logic to understand what is happening and thereby make meaning out of the situation. In this mode of decision-making action follows thought. We can only insert the pause if there is no emotional charge associated with the memories that are triggered by events in the outside world.

In conscious belief-based decision-making we have time to think about what decision to make, and we have time to discuss with others and build consensus. However, conscious belief-based decision-making has one thing in common with subconscious belief-based decision-making: it uses information based on past experiences to make decisions about the future. It creates a future very much like the past. At the best, the future we create is only incrementally different. We are using our beliefs based on past experiences to design our future experience.

Enabling leaders, managers and employees to make the shift from subconscious belief-based decision-making to conscious belief-based decision-making should be the purpose of personal alignment or personal transformation programmes. We are attempting to uncover and release the limiting beliefs that cause emotional upset and prevent leaders, managers and employees from fully living their own values and the organisation's values.

These are also the limiting beliefs that are the root cause of much of the cultural entropy.

Values-based decision-making

If we truly want to create the future we want to experience, we have to shift from conscious belief-based decision-making to values-based decision-making. That is not to say there is no place for conscious belief-based decision-making based on logic and rational thinking. There is. However, all critical decisions need to pass the values test. The question we need to ask when making a decision is "Is this decision rational *and* is it in alignment with our values?" If it isn't in alignment with your values then you should think again.

A decision that is not in alignment with the organisation's espoused values lacks integrity. A decision that is not in alignment with your personal values lacks authenticity. You cannot create personal or group cohesion by making decisions that lack authenticity and integrity. We make values-based decisions so that we can create the feeling we want to experience. If we value trust, then we make decisions that allow us to display and feel trust. If we value accountability, then we make decisions that allow us to display and feel accountable.

When we make values-based decisions, we consciously create the future we want to experience. When we hold a vision, we consciously make decisions that keep us heading in that direction. When we have a mission, we consciously make decisions that support the attainment of that mission. In every case we are making decisions that help us consciously create the future we want to experience. Values-based decision-making is different from conscious belief-based decision-making in that it deemphasises meaning-making. In other words, we are not attempting to match up packages of information that represent our current experience with the packages of information stored in our memory so that we can release instructions based on past experiences.

We are taking the packages of information that are created by the brain and examining them in our minds without any predetermined judgement about how we should respond. We are effectively saying to ourselves "How can we respond to this situation in such a way that we are able to express our values?" We are trying to let our values guide our behaviour, not our beliefs. Values are universal concepts that transcend all contexts. Beliefs on the other hand are local and contextual.

What is remarkable is that organisations that live by their values are among the most successful organisations on the planet. This is the key theme in most successful company turn-arounds. It is one of the principal conclusions in Collins and Porras's book *Built to Last: Successful Habits of Visionary Companies*. Successful long-lasting companies live their values. It is also one of our major findings based on eight years of working with the Seven Levels of Consciousness model and the Cultural Transformation Tools. We have found that the most successful companies display full-spectrum consciousness—they operate with positive values at every level of consciousness.

Characteristics of Intuition-based decision-making

The principal characteristics of intuition-based decision-making are as follows:

1. Data gathering and information processing take place in the normal way;
2. Judgement is suspended; no meaning-making takes places, subconscious or conscious;
3. The mind is empty; thoughts, beliefs and agendas are suspended;

4. The mind is free to make a deep dive into the mind-space of the collective unconscious;
5. After a period of reflection, thoughts arise that are based on a deep sense of knowing; and
6. The thoughts reflect wisdom; they focus on the common good; they are in alignment with our most deeply held values; and they give consideration to the long-term. They reflect what wants to emerge.

For most organisations, the shift from belief-based decision-making to values-based decision-making is already a stretch. The subsequent shift from values-based decision-making to intuition-based decision-making is for many a bridge-too-far. However, it is not necessarily a bridge-too-far for the more evolved leaders or managers in an organisation—those that have developed full-spectrum personal consciousness. What is different in this mode of decision-making is that there is no conscious or subconscious attempt at meaning-making, *and* there is no focus on the past or the future.

The decision arises out of "presence" in the current moment. Beliefs lead to decisions based on past experiences. Values lead us to decisions based on the feelings we want to experience in the future. Intuition allows us to create a future based on the emergence of being. When we create the conditions that allow our minds to tap into the collective mind-space, our intuition informs us of what wants or needs to emerge.

PERSONAL VALUES AND DECISION-MAKING

To discuss personal values and decision-making, we need to be clear about what we mean. The dictionary definition of value is 'A principle, standard, or quality considered worthwhile or desirable.' Values are a major motivating force for people because they categorise how people attach meaning, worth and importance to things. When a person's values are matched, they feel complete and satisfied. If values are not met, there is a sense of dissatisfaction, unease or incongruity. This is something to bear in mind during persuasion and negotiation.

Examples of values are health, pleasure, recognition, safety, integrity, achievement and honesty. These are all quite subjective terms, which means that they may mean different things to different people. Or even different things to the same person at different times.

So how are personal values and decision-making related? Our personal values very much determine our goals and outcomes in life. The goals we choose are the outer expression of our personal values. And decision-making is similarly based upon our core values. For a start, even choosing your goals is decision-making! A person's values will determine how they perceive any particular situation. Someone who values 'safety' will approach a situation checking for safety versus danger.

A person who values 'excitement' will have a different perspective on the same situation and will be searching for different kinds of experiences. So you understand how personal values and decision-making drive each other. The values determine the outcomes set and the decision-making designed to achieve them. The decision-making, in turn, is organised to ensure the personal values are matched.

So how can we benefit from this interaction between personal values and decision-making? Well firstly, if you want to know what your personal values are, you only need to think about some of the decisions you have made. What was important to you at the time? What other factors did you consider? Of all these factors, which was most important? Least important? Sometimes it's easier for other people to point out to you what they think your values are. It may be helpful to you to ask others about your personal values and decision-making.

Why? Because when you know what you're personal values are, your decision-making becomes infinitely easier.

A person's identity and personality is 'held together', you could say, by their values and beliefs. And we know your personal values and decision-making are intimately connected. Knowing how to make decisions that satisfy your personal values means that your sense of self is strengthened by every decision. As opposed to making decisions that somehow weaken or fragment who you are. Consider how this might happen in a group, where different people hold different values that are at odds with each other. Or even the same value, but expressed differently.

Unless there's a fundamental shift, any decision will mean that somebody's values are not being met. A useful strategy here is to get each member to identify with particular shared values. Defining shared values is a powerful method to generate cohesion in groups. Similarly, knowing your own values means that should there ever be a conflict, you can quickly and easily reorganise your value set to allow you to make an effective decision.

In terms of learning about your personal values and decision-making, it is possible to spend a lot of time trying to work out your values, taking tests, re-evaluating them and so on. And your time would not have been best spent. There have also been times in your life when all your values are completely aligned. You have a deep felt sense of who you are, knowing what's a match for your personal values and decision-making is effortless for you. Learning about and knowing how to establish this position for yourself is personally very powerful. It allows you to easily reorganise your personal values and decision-making takes on a whole new dimension for you.

MAKING GOOD DECISIONS

You make many, many decisions every day. What you have for breakfast, which shoes to put on, which shops to browse in, who to spend time with, and sometimes even what you do at work. Some decisions are one off's, for example, do you go to the party tonight, or not? Other decisions you make once, and they carry forward in time.

For example you decide that you like a particular TV series and you plan to watch it every week. And it's not that you decide every week that you going to watch it. You decide only once, and every week you carry out the result of that decision. If you haven't read the overview of the model, it may be useful to do so now before continuing with 'how do I make good decisions?'

Good and Bad Decisions

There are times when you have made excellent decisions. You knew coming up to it more or less what you were going to decide. At the time of the decision-making you knew it was a good decision. And when you look back on it you recognise that, yes, that was a good decision. And even now you still think it is a good decision and it holds true even today. There are also times when you made decisions that you felt uneasy about.

Even if you asked yourself how do I make good decisions, there still may have been a sense that there was something not quite right about your decision-making. And even when you look back on it you recognise that at the time you realised it was a poor decision with the associated negative consequences. So when you think about how do make good decisions with the above in mind, what do we know? We know that there is some information present in the system at the time of making the decision that lets you know whether it is a good or bad decision. This information is also available when you think back to the time of making the division.

If you knew what this information was, then you'd be able to answer the question 'how do I make good decisions?' Some people refer to a 'gut feeling' or a 'heart-felt' sense, some kind of sensation in the body. Others refer to hearing a voice giving them advice or talking to themselves. And yet others talk about a flash of inspiration, or seeing the whole picture. A visual cue.

Whether it's a visual, sensory, or auditory signal that the person is aware of, this is simply the information that's available to them at the time. Each of us is using all our five senses on an ongoing basis. Typically though, an individual may be aware of only one or maybe two of these at any one time. The other information will become available if you simply put your attention on it. So how does this apply to your question of how do I make good decisions? Well, it's the awareness of this very information in the system that actually lets you know whether it is a good decision or a bad decision.

If you want to know your own personal signals for how do I make good decisions, try this experiment. Think of something that you really do not like. For example, filling in tax forms, muddy footprints in the house, very loud noises, something that you do not like. When you think about this thing, how is it that you know that you do not like it? What are you aware of in your body as a sensation that lets you know you do not like it?

Do you have an image in your mind's eye of this particular thing? If you were to point to it, where would you point? Just notice the location in space of this picture and whether it is black and white or colour, a movie or a slide, how big it is and so on. And when you talk to yourself about not liking this thing, notice where the voice inside originates from? Notice also the tonality and the rate of speech. Now think of something that you really do enjoy. Something that gives you a lot of pleasure, that is pleasing to you to spend time at. This will generate different sensations in your body. Notice for yourself where they are and what the sensations are.

When you visualise the thing in your mind's eye the picture will typically be in a different place. Notice the qualities of the picture. And when you talk to yourself about this thing that you really like, this voice will be different from the last one. It may be different tonality, different volume, different speed and it may even originate from a different location. This is how your system holds things that it likes and dislikes. Things that are a aligned with it and things that are not. There will also be a separate set of signals and information about things that are neutral, things about which you don't know.

When you're making your decisions it is similar information that is present in the system that lets you know whether it's a good decision for you or not. Whether it's for you or not. You actually have your own yes no guide to better decisions built in! Paying attention to the signals at the time of your decision-making means that you get to make the choices that are appropriate for you.

And the bonus is that you have confidence that you're making a good decision. If it's a bad decision you simply readjust and alter your decision on the spot. You don't have to wait for all those negative consequences to know it was a bad decision! So there's your answer to 'How do I make good decisions?'

If you want to turbo charge your decision-making it's useful to include yourself in the decision-making process. By this I mean you not only consider what to be doing, but your decision-making model includes who you are and specifically how to keep that intact without compromise.

FASTER DECISION-MAKING

If you want to know how to make faster decisions, you need some kind of decision-making system in place. And like any other system, when it works smoothly and easily it becomes more efficient. This means, of course, that the first thing to do is to put a system in place.

I know, I know! Some of you may have been hoping to skip this step. But before you do anything, consider this. Do you want to know how to make faster decisions because you need to make a particular decision quickly and you're prepared to put up with whatever long-term consequences come along?

Or do you want to put a solid decision-making model in place that will teach you how to make faster decisions that work every time? Where not only the short-term but also the long-term consequences are in your favour? If it's the former, I have found just the thing for you! A decision-making novelty! It would actually be funny except for the fact that some people actually live their lives this way! If you want to know how to make faster decisions using a dependable decision-making model and you are also committed to having a life that works on many levels.

If you're in a bad state, and you're having a bad day, you make bad decisions. If you're having a great day, and you're in a great state, you make great decisions. You also know how to make faster decisions using your own reliable decision-making model. So it makes sense to make sure you're in a great state. And if you know how to make sure you're in a great state, why would you not choose to be this way all the time? So let's consider what you're like...

There are times when you're in great form, when everything is going your way. There's a sense of being calm... at peace... and at ease. You feel relaxed and ready for whatever happens... There is an overall sense of well-being and satisfaction. It's as if all you have to do is to turn up, and things happen for you. Things that were problematic before are now different. Everything is right with the world and things work out for you. People often describe it as feeling light, walking tall, or being on top of the world. For athletes, it's being 'in the zone'.

Other people may bring to you things that for them are a problem. And in an instant, you have a solution that works easily and quickly. Like this, you naturally know how to make faster decisions. Some of you may be thinking that this is all well and good, but it doesn't happen very often for you. This may be true, and when you are this way, even if it's only for a moment, there is something magnificent about it.

You feel whole, complete and internally aligned. Mentally, emotionally and physically you are operating as a single unit. You are very much in the present... and at the same time, moving into your future... Your whole system is centered and grounded... and simultaneously any action or movement is done with the least amount of energy needed... You are relaxed... and ready...

So consider for yourself what it's like when you are this way. Give yourself a couple of seconds, pause for a moment, and notice what it's like for you...

Chances are, to even consider this, you moved your physical body in some way. It may be that you sat back, that you set up straighter, or you relaxed your shoulders, or took a breath in a certain way. But you made some kind of postural adjustment. The particular adjustment that you made is how you access the operating position that I've been referring to. You move your physical body, and it has an impact on your system.

Most people are acutely aware of the various muscle tension and aches they have when they are stressed. They are not usually aware of their muscle tone and level of relaxation that is present when your system is operating at its optimum. Learning what this position feels like, and learning how to access it, is incredibly useful. Not only do you know how to make faster decisions, but the way you perceive the world shifts. For a start, your attention is no longer on problems and difficulties. Instead you attend to what is working and what is possible for you.

All your past experiences, learnings and resources are instantly available to you. So all this knowledge and information is present when you come to actually make decisions, when you're going through the process of decision-making. The preparation, of course, is in setting up the starting position. Oftentimes it easier to have somebody else point out to you the movements that you make.

However, the time and effort is well spent. Once you know how to access this position it is always available to you. It becomes a matter of simply choosing to access this position. And from here you invariably make good decisions. Decisions that are beneficial to you and those around you, both in the immediate future as well as into the distant future.

And with a little practice, the whole decision-making process becomes very fast. And even though you may make faster decisions than before, you are assured that they are appropriate for you in terms of getting what you want. Using this particular model to know how to make faster decisions with confidence also means that you get to strengthen your operating position. Because it's built into the model. It's not just an aspect of this decision-making model, it's the basis upon which this decision-making model is structured.

3

DECISION-MAKING STYLES

As a leader you're stuck with decision-making. It's your job to make decisions that are in the best interest of the whole organisation. You must consider the good of many, not of a few. This is a big responsibility and very often people don't appreciate your efforts. In fact, many times people get angry at you because of the decisions you make to help them! Let's take a moment and discuss decision-making style. Not the decision itself, but style. As you read the descriptions below, consider the style you most often use and ask yourself if you consistently use the proper style for each situation.

Democratic decision-making is when the leader gives up ownership and control of a decision and allows the group to vote. Majority vote will decide the action. Advantages include a fairly fast decision, and a certain amount of group participation. The disadvantage of this style includes no responsibility. An individual is not responsible for the outcome. In fact, even the group feels no real responsibility because some members will say, "I didn't vote for that." Lack of group and personal responsibility seems to disqualify this style of decision-making; however, the democratic style does have its place in business.

Autocratic decision-making is when the leader maintains total control and ownership of the decision. The leader is also completely responsible for the good or bad outcome as a result of the decision. The leader does not ask for any suggestions or ideas from outside sources and decides from his or her own internal information and perception of the situation. Advantages include a very fast decision, and personal responsibility by the leader, for the outcome. If an emergency situation exists, the autocratic style is usually the best choice.

The disadvantages are varied and sometimes include less than desired effort from the people that must carry out the decision. If the employee is personally affected by the decision but not included when the decision is made, morale and effort may or may not suffer. It is not always predictable. If the outcome for the decision is not positive, members of the organisation begin to feel they could have done a better job themselves and the leader may lose credibility.

Participative decision-making is when the leader involves the members of the organisation. Other perspectives of the situation are discovered because the leader deliberately asks and encourages others to participate by giving their ideas, perceptions, knowledge, and information concerning the decision. The leader maintains total control of the decision because, although outside information is considered, the leader alone decides. The leader is also completely responsible for the good or bad outcome as a result of the decision.

The advantages include some group participation and involvement. This is especially valuable when a person is affected negatively by the decision. In most cases, the individual is informed before the decision is implemented (no surprises) and usually feels good about personal involvement. If the leader is a good communicator, and listens carefully to the information collected, he or she will usually have a more accurate understanding of the situation and make a better decision. The disadvantages of this style include a fairly slow, time consuming decision; less security, because so many people are involved in the decision.

Consensus decision-making is when the leader gives up total control of the decision. The complete group is totally involved in the decision. The leader is not individually responsible for the outcome. The complete organisation or group is now responsible for the outcome. This is not a democratic style because everyone must agree and "buy in" on the decision. If total commitment and agreement by everyone is not obtained the decision becomes democratic.

The advantages include group commitment and responsibility for the outcome. Teamwork and good security is also created because everyone has a stake in the success of the decision. A more accurate decision is usually made, with a higher probability of success, because so many ideas, perspectives, skills and "brains" were involved in the creation. The disadvantages include a very slow and extremely time consuming decision. It is also a lot of work getting everyone in the organisation involved. It takes skill and practice for a group to learn how to work together.

ADJUSTING THE DECISION-MAKING STYLE

When we began our research, we expected to find that managers' predominant decision-making styles would change as they progressed through their careers. But the patterns that jumped right out of the data were even more sharply defined than we could have imagined. We found that decision-making profiles do a complete flip over the course of a career: That is, the decision style of a successful CEO is the opposite of a successful first-line supervisor's.

In the leadership (public) mode, we see a steady progression as managers move up in the ranks toward openness, diversity of opinion, and participative decision-making, matched by a step-by-step drop in the more directive, command-oriented styles.

In the thinking (private) mode, we see a progression toward the maximising styles where an executive prefers to gather a lot of information and think things through—and, at the highest executive levels, an uptick in the styles favouring one course of action.

There's a logic as well as an interdependence to the way the two aspects of decision-making evolve. As you move up the ladder, you move further and further away from where the action takes place, so it is easy to lose touch with what's really going on in the organisation. It's essential to use a leadership style that keeps the information pipeline open and the data flowing freely, so you have access to the best information and analysis. That's why the flexible and integrative styles dominate at the senior executive level.

The open pipeline in turn feeds the evolving thinking style, where the ever more analytic, information-hungry senior executive is focused on finding the single right answer. In public, the senior executive presents a willingness to consider options so as to encourage people to offer information. In private, he or she uses that information to zero in on a single option or, at a minimum, to narrow the options down to a workable strategy. These patterns in both public and private decision styles become even more pronounced when you isolate the most successful managers, who become even more open and interactive in their leadership styles and even more analytic in their thinking styles as they progress in their careers.

In both the public and the private modes, decision styles tend to cluster early in the management hierarchy. Somewhere between the manager and director levels, executives find that approaches that used to work are no longer so effective. At this point, we see managers' styles falling into a "convergence zone," where no one style stands out as being used more or less than the others. From then on, decision styles fan out again, though in the opposite direction, with different styles prevailing. The most successful managers come to the convergence zone more quickly than the least successful, our research reveals, and continue to adjust their styles as their careers progress.

The least successful seem to stagnate once they hit the convergence zone; their styles remain clustered rather than evolving in new directions. It appears that even though the least successful people do notice, at around the director level, that something has changed, they can't figure out what they should do differently. So they try a little of everything: Their styles are directive yet participative, action focused yet open to alternatives. The bottom 20 percent of managers get stuck in this "uncertainty zone," where they often remain for the rest of their careers.

The second level of management is a key transition point in an up-and-coming executive's career. At lower levels, the priority is to keep everyone focused on immediate tasks and getting the work done. At higher levels, that doesn't work anymore. Decision styles become more about listening than telling, more about understanding than directing.

Managers must drop the attachment to the hard-edged decisive and hierarchic modes of leadership in favour of the more inclusive flexible and integrative styles. This is a perilous time, a point where many otherwise talented managers crash and burn, because it's natural to keep doing things the way that worked well in the past.

We saw the impact of this transition in the case of Saurab, a second-level manager for a large petrochemical company. When we initially met Saurab, he was a first-line supervisor in a power-generation facility at the company. When we met him again, he had earned an MBA and was managing a department that functioned as a liaison between an operating unit and company headquarters. In a casual conversation, Saurab told us that he was enjoying the job—now that he had figured things out.

At first, he had found his new responsibilities confusing and distressing. But one morning he realised that although he had important things to do that day, none of them had to be resolved immediately. He could take some time, collect information, and seriously consider his choices. This was in sharp contrast with his previous job, where every day things had to be decided and done on the spot. Just recognising the difference eased the stress considerably and opened Saurab's eyes to the change needed in the way he handled decisions.

We see a secondary transition point taking place in the thinking styles of managers around the mid-executive and director levels. This is where the integrative style reaches its zenith, a time when managers must think creatively and float a range of ideas to be passed upstairs for consideration.

Beyond the director level, the pressure to think in an exploratory and creative way drops off, and more focused thinking again becomes important for success. Increasingly, managers must narrow down their choices and commit people and resources to particular plans. They are ultimately responsible for their decisions; they must be able to call the shots and—in rare instances—call them on the spot.

AUTHORITATIVE DECISION-MAKING STYLE

Authoritative decision-making is one decision-making style utilised by leaders. If it becomes the default and is the one method a leader uses, it can cause serious problems. In any particular situation, it's useful to have a range of different strategies to choose from. Other decision-making styles include facilitative, consultative and delegative.

The authoritative decision-making style is useful when the leader possesses all the necessary information and has the required expertise to make the best decision. He/she makes the decision and the subordinates are then informed of what the decision is. This style is useful when the leader is the expert, and when a fast decision is required. The leader takes sole responsibility for the decision.

Depending on the situation, this aspect could actually be listed under both pros and cons! The authoritative decision-making style is least useful when there is expertise available elsewhere that the leader could call on to make a more effective decision. Nor is it useful if it becomes the only decision-making style used by power driven individuals.

Facilitative Decision-making Style

The facilitative decision-making style indicates a joint effort between leaders and subordinates, both providing input to make a shared decision. It is important that subordinate have access to the information required to make the decision. They should also have some degree of expertise and/or motivation to ensure the best decision is made. Responsibility for this decision is shared and this style can actually be very empowering to subordinates, unlike the authoritative decision-making style which can have quite the opposite effect. The facilitative style is useful when the risks of a poor decision are minimal and the benefits of including the subordinates are significant, such as arranging timetables, or benefit programmes.

Consultative Decision-making Style

Consultative decision-making is said to occur when the leader asks for advice and opinions from his subordinates, and makes the decision himself. As in the authoritative decision-making style, responsibility remains with the leader. If the subordinates have expertise or information that will help make a more effective decision, a wise leader will ask for it. But unless the subordinates understand that that's what is occurring, it can lead to upset or disappointment.

Delegative Decision-making

Delegative decision-making, as the name implies, is when a leader passes responsibility for the decision-making and the decision to one or more subordinates. It may even be all the subordinates. Again, the pros and cons are determined by the expertise and knowledge of those actually making the decision. The style obviously comes into its own as the organisation gets larger, and means the leader does not necessarily have to make all the decisions.

Flexibility

A good leader will move easily between the styles

depending on context. It takes quite a degree of awareness of self, as well as an understanding of the limits of your own expertise, to be flexible in this way.

Effects

It is said that authoritative decision-making gives rise to decisions that get things done. However, the results are short lived unless there is a sense of legitimacy about the decisions. In other words, the appropriate relationship exists between the decision-maker and the subordinates. Studies also suggest that authoritative decision-making by mothers shows up as higher grade point averages and less occurrence of risky behaviours in European and American adolescents.

DECISION-MAKING MODELS

The many decision-making models that exist nowadays means that you even have to make a decision as to which one to use! There are rational models, intuitive models, rational-iterative models as well as 5, 6, 7 and even 9 step decision models. Most, however, move through each of the basic stages in decision-making. Some of these decision-making models presuppose that decision-making is the same as problem solving. Frequently, the first step in the decision-making process is to identify the problem.

Decision-making is about choosing from several options or ideas and taking action to generate a particular result. It is usually considered to be a rational and logical thinking process. However, this does not explain the decision-making process in every case. Sometimes you will hear people saying things such as 'I listened to my heart' or 'I went with my gut'. Obviously, they are using a different approach.

Stages in Decision-Making

Of the stages in decision-making, this is probably the most significant step. It is vital to have a good understanding and be very clear about:

1. The situation and
2. What you want to achieve.

Any misinformation about the situation is likely to be amplified in the later stages in decision-making. For example, a passerby who considers the unconscious person on the street to be a drunk will act differently than if they knew that person was actually suffering a stroke.

Being clear about what you want the decision to achieve will also have knock on effects on the later stages in decision-making. It's very easy to know what is not wanted, e.g., 'I don't want this anymore', or 'This has to stop'. But such framing of the outcome in the negative does not set a direction to move towards, only what to move away from.

Instead, state in the positive what you want the decision to achieve. For example, instead of 'I want to stop wasting my time here' you could say 'I want to get this chapter finished in the next 2 hours.' This sets a very clear and measurable outcome for the decision-making process. It will often allow a much smoother transitioning through the subsequent stages in decision-making as well.

Alternatives

Unless you are choosing from alternatives there is no decision to make! The number of alternatives you choose will depend on such factors as experience, knowledge, skills, number of people involved in generating alternatives and what's considered important.

Information gathering

The information required can be about the alternatives or even about the situation and the required outcome. As alternatives are suggested, it may require further clarification of the situation or the decision to be made. Of the stages in decision-making, this one often takes the most time. An aspect of the rational decision-making models is the weighing up of the pros and cons of the various alternatives so as to arrive at the best.

As you may have experienced, this can take so long as to inhibit the decision-making process! In contrast, This can be one of the quickest stages of the recognition primed decision-making model, where the information gathering is done mentally by the expert by rapidly bringing his or her acquired experiences and skills to bear on the situation.

Selection

Selection is the choosing of one of the alternatives. Although it's listed as only one of the stages of decision-making, many people consider that this is the whole of the decision-making process. An idea that means that they pay little or no attention to the previous stages, which makes this one very tricky! However, if the previous stages of decision-making have been done well, this stage is actually fairly straightforward.

The method of selection will very much depend on the decision-making process. Rational decision models choose the option that has more pros than cons. Intuitive decision-makers 'go with their gut', or their heart. The ultimate decision-making model put forward in this web site selects based on what will allow you to be who you want to be, and what allows you to live your own life.

Action

It's important to include this in the stages of decision-making because any time spent making a decision is wasted if it is not converted into action. Great decisions are only great when they are carried into action and the action achieves the desired result. And an aspect of taking action is assessing whether the decision actually achieved the desired outcome. And if not, making modifications until it does so.

Stages in Decision-Making

The order of the stages in decision-making is important if you want to make quality decisions effortlessly and consistently. You won't know what information to gather unless you know what the situation is and what alternatives are being considered. It's difficult to select an option if you don't know what you are trying to achieve.

Remember, too, that it may be necessary to cycle back to an earlier stage when the information in the system changes. For example, having gathered some information, you may realise that it makes sense to update what you want the decision to achieve. Or taking action may give you an alternative not previously considered.

Rational Model

Rational decision-making models involve a cognitive process where each step follows in a logical order from the one before. There are different types of rational models and the number of steps involved, and even the steps themselves, will differ in different models. Some people assume that decision-making is equivalent to problem solving. Some decisions however are not problem oriented and describing the general outline of a rational model below.

Different Steps

1. Define the situation/decision to be made
2. Identify the important criteria for the process and the result
3. Consider all possible solutions
4. Calculate the consequences of these solutions versus the likelihood of satisfying the criteria
5. Choose the best option

The comparison is often performed by filling out forms or charts that have many names. Decision matrix, Pugh matrix, decision grid, selection matrix, criteria rating form, amongst others. A relative importance is given to each criterion and the options are scored against each of the criteria and the highest 'wins'.

Pros and Cons

A rational decision-making model presupposes that there is one best outcome. Because of this it is sometimes called an optimising decision-making model. The search for perfection is frequently a factor in actually delaying making a decision. Such a model also presupposes that it is possible to consider every option and also to know the future consequences of each.

While many would like to think they know what will happen, the universe often has other plans! It is also limited by the cognitive abilities of the person making the decision; how good is their memory? how good is their imagination? The criteria themselves, of course, will be subjective and may be difficult to compare. These models require a great deal of time and a great deal of information. And, of course, a rational decision-making model attempts to negate the role of emotions in decision-making.

Six Step Decision-making

The six step decision-making process is a rational decision making process. This means that it is based upon thinking about, comparing and evaluating various alternatives. Rational decision-making models are typically described as linear, sequential processes.

In other words, there are steps laid out for you to follow. Each step must be completed before you go to the next step. And occasionally it may be necessary to go back several steps to more fully complete them before you go forward again. There are various 6 step decision-making processes described and usually the steps are very similar, only the wording is different.

Steps

1. Define the situation and the desired outcome.
2. Research and identify options.
3. Compare and contrast each alternative and its consequences.
4. Make a decision and choose an alternative.
5. Design and implement an action plan.
6. Evaluate results.

Uses

Six step decision-making processes have been utilised extensively in organisations. Traditional ethical decision-making models can be incredibly complex. They have been simplified to a six step decision-making process so that employees can be empowered to make decisions appropriate to their rank and responsibility. It is also commonly used in schools to teach children how to make decisions.

Pros

Occasionally, clearly defining a situation and stating the required outcome can go a long way towards improving a situation. It is important regardless of the type of decision-making process. Researching all your options increases the amount of information in the system. This often gives rise to options previously not considered or may even generate options in regard to other unrelated decisions. It is often considered that complex situations often require complex decision-making processes. But is it not often the case that in a complex, chaotic situation.

Cons

A six step decision-making process can become a waste of time and energy and effort if there is too much attention to detail in researching options. If it leads to a delay in decision-making, there may be wasted opportunities and missed chances. Sometimes beliefs and assumptions are mistaken for facts with unwanted consequences.

The search for the best option instead of an effective one may mean even more time wasted, decisions not being made, and lost opportunities. The emphasis is on cognition, or thinking, and there is little consideration of the individual, or their internal body signals. Despite the fact that these kind or models are taught extensively, recent research shows that people don't actually make decisions this way. Up to 95 per cent of decisions are done differently!

Vroom-Jago Model

The Vroom-Jago decision model is a rational model used by leaders to determine whether they should make a decision alone or involve a group, and to what extent the group should be involved. This method was first proposed by Vroom and Yetton in 1973 and was later modified by Vroom and Jago in 1988.

Subsequent studies have shown that the greater precision in situational assessment of the Vroom-Jago decision model allows for better discrimination in choosing a process. In some business situations it's better for a leader to be the decision-maker for the group. In others, it's best for the group to have some input or even make the decision. This model distinguishes five different situations and outlines an algorithm for determining which one to use.

Five processes

1. *Autocratic l (Al)* You, the decision-maker, use the information available to make the decision yourself.
2. *Autocratic ll (A2)*You request information from members of your team. They may or may not know why you want such information. They neither define the situation, alternatives or final choice.
3. *Consultative l (Cl)* You explain the situation to the individual members of the group but they do not get together as a group. You make the final decision.
4. *Consultative ll (C2)* There is group discussion where you explain the situation and gather ideas and

suggestions. Again, you're responsible for the final decision-making.

5. *Group II (G2)* The group as a whole make the decision. You as the leader present the situation and the group defines alternatives and reaches a consensus decision. The leader acts more as a facilitator in this process and allows the group to agree on the final choice.

The Vroom-Jago decision model uses a series of seven questions, asked in order, to determine which of these five processes to use. This is a somewhat prescriptive process and allows you to move through the diagram below. On reaching the right-hand side, the indicated process is the most appropriate for your situation.

Seven questions

1. Is high quality important here or is a good solution absolutely critical?
2. As the leader, do you have enough information of your own to make a good decision?
3. Is the problem structured in that it is clearly defined, organised and has recognised solutions?
4. Do the members of the group have to accept this decision for it to work?
5. If you make this decision yourself, are you sure the group will accept it?
6. Are the group members aligned with the same goals that you are trying to achieve?
7. Is disagreement likely among group members in reaching a decision?

In the example, if the quality requirement is not high, choose the upper limb. With regards to question 4, if they have to accept it, choose 'yes'. Then 'yes' again if you know they will accept your decision. This points you at A1, so you go ahead and make the decision yourself.

Seven Step Model

It was designed for those who wanted a decision-making model to help with choosing a career path or deciding what to do about a job offer. An important factor in the model is information gathering. It is suggested that the more information that's available, the easier it is to make decisions. So many of the steps are designed to do just this.

Seven steps

1. Identify the decision to be made - exactly what are you trying to decide?
2. Know yourself - what are your strengths, weaknesses, skills, values and interests
3. Identify options - list the various choices so far
4. Gather information and data - about each alternative
5. Evaluate options that will solve the problem, pros, cons and risks of each alternative
6. Select the best option- may be necessary to loop back and gather more info
7. Develop a plan of action - and implement it!

Pros and cons

The 7 Step Decision-making Model was designed for career decision-making and so can be a bit cumbersome if applied to decisions that are not as significant. Not so useful for deciding between chocolate or vanilla ice cream, for example! Information overload may actually inhibit the decision-making, as well as trying to figure out which information is relevant and which is not. And this model is not how we as humans naturally make decisions.

The first step in the 7 Step Decision-making Model is very important, whatever decision you have to make. Sometimes just clarifying what the decision is, or what the question you want answered is, makes it much easier to decide.

Intuitive Models

Some people consider these decisions to be unlikely coincidences, lucky guesses, or some kind of new-age hocus-pocus. Many universities are still only teaching rational decision-making models and suggest that if these are not used, failure results. Some researchers are even studying the logic behind the intuitive decision-making models! The groups who study intuitive decision-making models are realising that it's not simply the opposite of rational decision-making. Carl Jung pointed out that it is outside the realm of reason.

In military schools the rational, analytical models have historically been utilised. It is also long been recognised, however, that once the enemy is engaged the analytical model may do more harm than good. History is full of examples where battles have more often been lost by a leader's failure to make a decision than by his making a poor one.

The military are educating the soldiers of every rank in how to make intuitive decisions. Information overload, lack of time and chaotic conditions are poor conditions for rational models. Instead of improving their rational decision-making, the army has turned to intuitive decision models because they work!

Recognition Primed Model

In 1985 Gary Klein and others began to develop the recognition primed decision-making model. They were studying decision-making in the army and were examining how firefighting chiefs make decisions. They realised that these expert decision-makers were not comparing lists of options. They were not even comparing two options. So they ended up revising the whole research project and came up with a model of how people actually make decisions.

In a given situation, the decision-maker will pick up cues and indicators that let them recognise patterns. Based on these patterns and the decision they have to make, the person chooses a single course of action, an 'action script', that they consider will achieve the outcome. Klein and Co. wondered how people could assess this single option if they were not comparing it to something else. What they found was that the decision-maker would run the action script through a mental simulation.

The mental simulation was based on mental models that the decision-maker had developed through experience. In other words, the decision-maker has an idea how things work based on the knowledge that has been gained from experience.She/ he compares the option against what is known to work.

If the decision-maker considers the action script will achieve the outcome, they go ahead. If they consider that it might not work because of a potential problem, they may try and alter the action script in some way. If mentally they don't think it will work, they discard it completely, and choose a second action script. This is then mentally rehearsed and so on until they find an action script that they think will work. This is then utilised. Note that in this recognition primed decision-making model there is no comparison of alternatives.

As people become more expert in their chosen field, as they have more and more experience, their ability to recognise patterns is enhanced. This gives them more options to choose from. Which means that, more often than not, the first option they choose will work. Their rapid and effective movement through the recognition primed decision-making model is what makes them experts.

Intuitive and Rational Model

What Klein and Co. are suggesting in their recognition primed decision-making model is the use of intuitive as well as rational decision-making models, but with our intuition in the driving seat! Intuition is used to recognise situations and help to decide how to respond, and analysis is used to verify that our intuitions are appropriate to the situation.

You might think that the recognition primed decision-making model will work for some decisions, but not for others. There are two things here. First of all, initially Klein suggested that 90 per cent of important decisions were probably made this way, with more than 90 per cent of routine decisions. Subsequent research has suggested that his initial ideas were actually biased in favour of rational decision-making. So he's probably actually underestimating how often people use a recognition primed decision-making process!

Secondly, if you're concerned about making major decisions in this way, Klein also found that army officers used intuition in 96 per cent of their planning decisions. Naval commanders used this model 95 per cent of the time, too. Commercial air crews and managers of offshore oil platforms use intuition in 90 per cent of their decisions!

The process of the recognition primed decision-making model is being used to replace the conventional army military decision-making process (MDMP) in many units. Why? Because it works! Plans using the recognition primed decision-making process are found to be bolder and better adapted to situational demands than the other plans. The army military decision-making process is supposed to enable an officer to develop tactically sound battle plans that result in success. It has also been found to have the opposite result in many cases! The recognition primed decision-making model is being advocated now in the global war on terrorism.

Pros

— It works!

— It's natural. And free of gluten, dairy and nuts.

Cons

Not enough people know about it. Which means the following things occur and recognition primed decision-making is not practiced:

1. People ignore feedback—or don't seek it out.
2. Rapid turnover of staff is allowed—Staff never get much experience in one area so decision-making effectiveness is not what it could be.
3. In our rapidly changing world, the latest models are quickly embraced to replace ones that actually work. The experience of the experts in the older working models is discounted. Paper credentials are becoming more important than experience. Procedures are instituted that don't properly capture the nuances of a situation.

These things prevent the pattern recognition necessary for recognition primed decision-making and actually hamper effective decision-making. There will be a price to pay!

ULTIMATE DECISION-MAKING MODEL

The decision-making process is very much determined by who you are. The way you are being in the world. Who you are determines not just what you think but how you think. This makes it incredibly important to establish your way of being before you even consider any kind of decision-making process.

So let's say, you know how to establish a sense of self that is whole and complete. You understand how to generate this position from within, you recognise the signals that let you know when you're operating from this position. Only then should you turn your attention to the decision-making process. There are a huge number of decision-making processes available to choose from. Where do you begin?

Some people use their intuition, others prefer a rational model, and of course, they will have lots of reasons as to why this is better! There are decision trees, decision maps, a variety of decision matrix and decision matrix tables and so on.

There are so many, in fact, it would be easy to be indecisive about which one to choose! And then of course there is the search for the best decision. This quest is often a major factor for people being indecisive and not making any decision at all.

Nine Step Decision-making Model

The 9 step decision-making model is proposed by David Welsh in his book *'Decisions, Decisions'*. He calls it a subjective expected utility maximisation process. A utility, he explains, is a technical term used by economists and philosophers to indicate happiness, pleasure or satisfaction.

Subjective indicates that it's your pleasure, and expected because it is satisfaction or pleasure that you don't yet have, but hope to get. He suggests that SEU maximisation is the ideal. Using the 9 step decision-making model allows you to consistently aim to maximise your pleasure, and will be better for you in the long run than making decisions in any other way.

Step 1—Identify your objective

What is it you wish to achieve?

Step 2—Do a preliminary survey of your options

Besides the most obvious choices available to you, what other kinds of options can you think of?

Step 3—Identify the implicated values

What values are at stake here? If it's an easy or unimportant decision you may not necessarily do this step. But if the decision has a major impact on your wealth, your health or self-respect, then it's useful to be aware of it.

Step 4—Assess the importance of the decision

The importance of the decision will determine how much you invest in it in terms of time, energy and money. The importance is determined by examining the implicated values. You may also have to consider the context here as well, a different situation or environment can mean that a decision that is often not very important can become very significant.

Step 5—Budget your time and energy

Having identified the main alternatives and the values, now decide on which time and energy to spend making the decision itself. More important decisions are given more time and energy. He suggests that busy people and nervous wrecks made worse decisions than other people.

Step 6—Choose a decision-making strategy

This step of the 9 step decision-making model involves making another decision. The time and energy you plan to devote will affect the strategy you choose. And because the strategy you choose may profoundly affect your decision it's important to choose an appropriate one.

Step 7—Identify your options

When you examine your options in more detail you may discover other options with different implicated values. He points out that occasionally you may have to go back to step three to five and make revisions. Sometimes outside expertise may be able to provide options that you haven't thought of.

Step 8—Evaluate your options

This is where you compare the options available to you. Again he suggests that seeking advice from an expert is often easier than making the decision on your own.

Step 9—Make your choice—on time, on budget

When you're finished doing the evaluation, you make your choice. He notes that people may still have difficulty at this stage because they fear the consequences of making a bad decision. A colleague of his was once told 'Relax, no matter what you choose, you will regret it.' He considers this timeless wisdom because it is almost always possible to regret the choices we make. He suggests that by rigidly sticking to a decision-making schedule and budget you will eventually tame the demon of regret.

Pros and cons

As well as the 9 step decision-making model, he explains how we get caught out by numbers, gamblers fallacy, as well as some of the other decision-making biases and mistakes that we are subject to as human beings. Step six and nine of this 9 step decision-making model seem to be tricky ones, the ones where you are actually choose between options! Step six to choose the strategy, and step nine to actually choose an option.

Of interest, too, is the idea that initially he says that self reflection is very important. However, in this 9 step decision-making model, there is no step that considers taking action, nor reviewing and assessing whether it was a good decision or not.

4

ROLE OF STRATEGIC THINKING IN DECISION-MAKING

Speechless thought moves over the fibres of our brain like water over the face of the deep. That we think, we know because we think. That we are, we know because we think; but what is it to think? And what is it to know that we think? What happens when you let your mind wander? When human mind has nothing specific to think about, it becomes chaotic, flitting from one thought to another in a random way. That's why thinkers are more often in a good mood while thinking than they are in their free time.

When one faces a problem, one must always ask whether the problem is thinkable. Not every idea or concept is thinkable. Moreover, every thinkable idea deserves its own duration of time in your mind. Our senses furnish the mind only with materials of information; it is our thinking that converts information we receive to our useful knowledge for decision-making. Decision-making is described as the economy of thinking. There are six steps that must be considered in making a good decision. The steps are as follows:

1. *Is it thinkable?* Is your problem thinkable?

2. *Is it my business?* Is it really necessary for you to think about it? It seems like one of the hardest lessons to be learned in life is where your business ends and somebody else's begins. The moment a question comes to your mind, see yourself mentally taking hold of it and disposing of it. In that moment is your choice made. You learn to become the decider and not the vacillator.
3. *Do you have enough explicit information to start your strategic thinking?* Information can be classified as explicit and tacit forms. The explicit information can be explained in structured form, while tacit information is inconsistent and fuzzy to explain. A good thinking resides in the capacity for evaluation of uncertain, hazardous, and conflicting information.
4. *How long should I think about it?* The key is in not "spending" time, but in "investing" it. Thinking does not stay in some minds very long because unfortunately they do not like solitary confinement that is needed. Decision does not just happen; it takes reflection and thought. Reflection time must be built into the decision process allowing ample time to ponder and rethink. For many people, unfortunately, the expectation that responding immediately is far more important than responding thoughtfully for many.
5. *Implementation*—Taking action. Thinking without action is daydreaming. To think too long about doing a thing often becomes its undoing.
6. *Monitoring my action*: Since everything changes, to be in control of my problem I have to adapt and update my thinking. The art of life is a constant readjustment to our situation.

Following the above thinking process with its many loops, then it is very likely that good ideas spring into being in response to your analytical probing. This analytical thinking is the most powerful tool for the mind. Without this, recurrence relation will keep coming back to your mind to haunt you. Mind maintains, and holds whatever has been put on it during the last few minutes. It holds and works on it, unless we replace by something new. Therefore, in order not to think about what is not worthy one must start thinking about something else immediately. That is the hygiene for the mind.

The crux is noticed in Alices' Adventures in Wonderland: " ' How am I to get in?' asked Alice again, in a louder tone. 'Are you to get in at all?' said the Footman, 'That's the first question, you know.'" Remember that most people waste most of their time every day majoring in minors. Time is of no account with great thoughts. Obviously, the basic problem is this: Law firms, which bill by the hour, are more profitable when less efficient.

As Goethe said, "Things, which matter most, must never be at the mercy of things which matter least." Time is the scarcest resource and unless it is managed nothing else can be managed. If you work on a nonexistent problem there are much fewer obstacles to overcome. To accomplish something noteworthy, we should look to do something worth the effort unless we are trying to relax. In times of leisure, nonexistent problems usually need to be sought out!

Here is an example of an unthinkable question/ problem. Is there an after life? This question is not thinkable. You must think about it as much as you think about "life before life." We can ask primal questions, but we can never stand near the beginning or the end. In other cases, the questions are thinkable, however, one "wishes" not even raise any doubt about them that invoke strategic thinking. These cases include, e.g., our deepest beliefs. And in many cases, one even deliberately changes the perception of the problem in order that it suits ones preconceived desirable decision. This is unfortunate, but people lie much more to themselves than to others.

As a general rule for strategic thinking, if you cannot describe in writing to be understood by someone else about your decision problem and what you are doing as a process about it, then you do not know what you are doing. The best place to make a decision is on paper. Being able to control the thought process is the hardest of all, and it takes discipline and training. One must develop the ability to engage in a consecutive, and a well-focused strategic thinking for a predetermined limited time in order produce a solution to a given well defined problem.

It is not that things will necessarily go wrong, but rather that they will take so much more time and effort than you think, if they are not to. The cardinal aim is to uncover the underlying logical structure of the decision problem by means of a mathematical model.

All branches of human knowledge are moving towards scientific representation. These include all the —logy subjects, such as sociology, and psychology, etc., usually being taught at our liberal art and humanity colleges. Nowadays, one expects a deeper understanding from studying sociometric, psychometric, and econometric, etc.

STRATEGIC DECISION

However, there is no expedient to which a man will not resort to avoid the real labour of thinking.

Remember that:

— Birds fly; when they get tired, they land.

— Man thinks; when he gets tired, he says "I understand."

Creativity: The fundamental project in life is engaging with the central idea that being strives for creativity. There are various ways in which being affirms the unlimited creative power. Moreover it dissolves whatever might restrict or mediate its expression, including the organisms, objects, representations, identities, and relations that this power generates along the way.

Thinking could be dangerous: The following metaphor illustrates how in some cases people prefer to not think for fear of being disappointed, adhering to the saying that "ignorance is bliss". There was a boy who lived his whole life on an iceberg. One day, he wondered what could be under the ice. He decided to dig in to find out for himself. To his greatest disappointment he discovered that he was actually living on water. From that day on, he never felt comfortable living on the iceberg and he wished he had not asked himself that question.

Mastering your fears: The major obstacle that stops people from making their own decisions is fear of making wrong decision.

When one has fear there are two primary reactions: facing the problem courageously or avoiding any commitments. However, since one has a powerful ability to analyse and understand, one can overcome the fear by self-psychoanalysis techniques to cope with the flight instinct. Top business performers have developed a multiple-step approach to conquering their fears. First, ask yourself a few important questions. Try to identify what you actually fear. Ask yourself what's the worst that can happen if you fail.

Most of the time in business, it's either a fear of loss or a fear of embarrassment. Next, identify what you could gain if the task or strategy works out well. This positive vision helps overshadow the negative fear. Last, ask yourself what the price is to you and to others if you do not overcome this fear. There are two types of people: those who try, stumble and get up and try again, and those who fear stumbling and never even try. Guess which type is more successful.

Our stomach is wiser than our brain: When one eats too much, the stomach rejects it by throwing up. However, the brain has no such mechanism. While mind controls the body, unfortunately, it is unable to control or give order to itself. The main cause for this is our habits, which are the centres of the gravity of the mind. Habits are weighing our mind down and therefore they are shortcuts that become comfortable means to avoid thinking.

Process of thinking for yourself : Thinking for yourself has been valued ever since ancient time.

The critical thinking techniques enable us to evaluate arguments and question the quality of the reasoning that leads to a certain conclusion. Too often we accept what we see and hear, becoming passive absorbers of information rather than critical listeners or readers. We must guard our mind against adapting a belief as our own before examining the validity of arguments for or against. We should ask questions in order to reach our own personal opinion or decision including:

1. What are the issue and conclusion?
2. What are the reasons?
3. Which words or phrases are ambiguous?
4. What are the value conflicts and assumptions?
5. What are the descriptive assumptions?
6. Are there any fallacies in the reasoning?
7. How good is the evidence?

8. Are there rival causes?
9. Are the statistics deceptive?
10. What significant information is omitted?
11. What reasonable conclusions are possible?

Unfortunately, pure uncritical thinking enables us to absorb a great deal of information and provides a foundation for more complex thinking at some future time. However, it is a passive exercise and, therefore, does not require an exhaustive mental effort, just concentration and memory skills. Clearly, this approach does not provide us with a method for discerning the facts, which could have serious consequences.

On the other extreme is the interactive approach to thinking that requires a "question-asking attitude" to determine the value of what is read and heard. If we are capable of thinking for ourselves, then the rewards are considerable and allows us to critically evaluate and then form personal opinions based on that evaluation of what makes sense and what is non-sense. We must also be aware that we bring our own personal experiences and values into the process and must not allow emotional involvement to taint our ability to think in an open-minded manner.

HOW TO IMPROVE YOUR THINKING SKILLS?

The many debates over mind and matter cover much of the history of human thoughts. The main engaging question, prior to the age of Enlightenment was how a nonphysical (i.e., mind) causes a physical (e.g., movements)?

Both Spinoza and Freud among others, worked on the unity of mind and body together with their interaction with nature and society. Spinoza was the first to question the concept of mind-and-body, i.e., physical and nonphysical duality dominated humanity for over twenty centuries.

He recognised that there is no such separation, but a manifestation of two different moods of the same thing. For example, when you have sufficient physical energy, then your mind registers it as feeling joyful. Anybody old enough has physical scars from all sorts of things. It is the same with the mind.

Humankind and nature: Genetic engineering has shown how it is possible to splice genes from one animal to another and not just animals. So, are humans really that unique? And even if they are not, are they that special? When one talks about humankind it is often with a tendency to separate man from the rest of animals. However, in reality there no such separation, the man is wholly nature not a kingdom within a kingdom. Humankind is not the crown and the hidden purpose of evolution.

According to the primatology, which has mounted ever more convincing bodies of evidence that there is really nothing special or unique about the human at all, that almost everything that you care to name is, to some degree or another, performed by other primates; it is all a matter of degree. And so, rather than distinct categories primatologists would rather have shifting shades of gray in the primate world and extend the term homo to a much broader population.

Nature of the man: Man has no nature, but he has history. In man the creature and the creator are one. While man is still undetermined animal, he is the strongest of all animals. What Nietzsche realised was that man must understand that life is not governed by rational principles. Life is full of cruelty, injustice, uncertainty and absurdity. There are no absolute standards of good and evil which can be demonstrated by human Reason.

There is only naked man living alone in a godless and absurd world. Modern industrial, bourgeois society made man decadent and feeble because it made man a victim of the excessive development of the rational faculties at the expense of human will and instinct. The task is to rediscover beneath all flattering colours and make-up the frightful fixed-text homo natura, which means: To translate man back into nature; to become master over the many vain and overly enthusiastic interpretations and connotations that have so far been scrawled and painted over that eternal basic text of homo natura.

To bring it about that man shall henceforth stand before man as he now, hardened by the discipline of science, stands before the other forms of nature. He is, in truth, anything but the crown of creation: beside him stand many other animals, all at similar stages of development.

Humankind and society: When man found himself bounded within the wall of society, all his instinct had to be broken to be replaced by the social norms. However, not all the instinct gave up their demand easily. The two most pervasive of all are: Anger, and Reproduction. Man derives the highest pleasure from sexual fulfilment, says Freud, but unconstrained sexuality drains the individual of psychic energy needed for a creative and intellectual life. Hence, it was society, working through the family, the priest, the teacher and the police, who imposes rules and restricts our animal nature which, because it is animal, demands release.

Such an existence is painful and so causes anxiety and frustration. But the violation of the rules of civilisation also gives us guilt. Either way, we suffer torment and pain. Civilised life simply entails too much pain for people. It seemed, for Freud, that the price we pay for civilisation is neuroses. Man has to find some sublimated means of satisfying the instinct.

For example, our sexual fulfilment is allowed by means of engaging in e.g., "Passionate-dancing", which is accompanied by the feeling and imagination of making love in bed but vertically. There are many other "acceptable means" for sexual fulfilment, such as sexual virtual-reality as a substitute for the real-reality.

Humankind and the self: We are particularly interested in the relation between anthropology and psychology. The difficulty of the Anthropology is how to articulate an analysis of what Homo Natura is on the basis of a definition of man as subject of liberty. More specifically, in its pragmatic character, the Anthropology aims to study what man makes of himself. So the realm of its investigation will neither be morality, metaphysics, nor the society, but what makes man, — or what he can and should do of himself.

Foucault observed that even though the anthropology posits man neither as homo natura nor as subject of freedom, but rather as he is given within the already operating syntheses of his relation with the world, i.e. as a citizen of the world, he/she then goes on to understand the dynamic of the inner sense. Nature proceeds throughout the whole infinite series of its possible determinations without outward incentive; and the succession of these changes is not arbitrary, but follows strict and unalterable laws.

Whatever exists in Nature necessarily exists as it is. Nature's relation to human beings is neutral while human's relation to nature is very complex process and yet undetermined. Consider for example in the animal kingdom, all creatures are striving to eat, survive, and reproduce. However, when it comes to man, he wonders and hopelessly looking for hidden purpose "as if" nature has a purpose.

Behavioural and brain sciences: It is a fact that humankind use crude information, such as colours, sounds, etc., in the environment in order to behave in a certain way. When forms of energy we call "stimuli" impinge on us our response begins. Creating an inner copy of the information, which is a representation of reality, does this. However this representation is at the service of the "will" in determining our behaviour.

In recent years there have been more interesting studies on the static geometry, i.e., the anatomy of the brain, leading to important testable predictions. However, the valuable progress in the brain/mind problem should be a comparative study in discovering relations between the physical dynamical structures generated by brain activity and the mental/conceptual structures. This includes the topology of subjective time and its alterations in psychopathology.

The brain is made up of billions of nerve cells. The portion of the brain responsible for thought and memory consists primarily of nerve cells, or neurons. Each neuron has three parts, dendrites (inputs), a cell body, and an axon (output) as shown below:

Neurons

The dendrites connect to the axons of other neurons. When these other neurons are stimulated, the dendrites convey the signal to the cell body via a synapse or connection, which either excites or inhibits the neuron with a different strength for each synapse:

When the excitation sufficiently outweighs inhibition, the neuron "fires". This sends a signal down its axon, which in turn excites or inhibits other neurons, and perhaps causes a muscle to move.

For at least three reasons, we are interested in knowing how our mind works:

— Better decisions are made by knowing the mechanism of our mind.

— Happiness or unhappiness are the states of mind.

— A better understanding of the mind can lead to setting new priorities as to what is taught/learned.

— Mind is what your brain does consciously, recall the often used phrases such as: never mind!, mind the gap, or mind your own business. A strategic thinking process is a neural network process inside our brains through many functional layers.

The following figure depicts the brain and mind functionality:

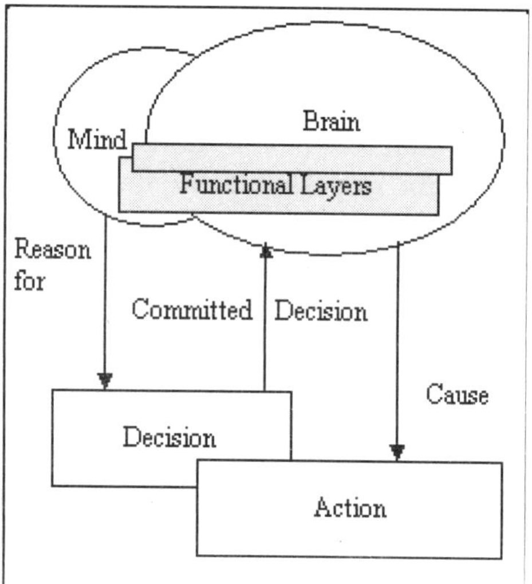

Modelling Process in Decision-Making

Figure. 4.1

The focal point of practical reasoning is action, as the focal point of empirical reasoning is observation. Perceptual takings or 'judgements' are the thoughts which typically arise from the impact of the world on our mind through our sensory capacities. Consciousness thinking is self-knowledge, that is, knowing what you know. Moreover, the process of becoming conscious distributes what you know throughout your brain via the brain neural network branches, i.e., chains of thought.

Unlike the connectivity between only two nodes of the network, the availability, and therefore expansion, of what you know throughout your neural network branches makes the information processing of your brain accurate. Thus, you possess a reflective, brilliant mental model of reality. However, one must be cautioned that the way we choose to see the world creates the world we see.

It is necessity to integrate your observations, your experiences, and your knowledge into a mental model. Your duty is whether the model is true or false, whether it represents reality rationally. Unfortunately, it might be a grab-bag of notions snatched at random, whose sources, validity, context and consequences you do not know, notions which, more often than not, you would drop like a hot potato if you knew. Human beings are basically electrochemically driven membrane processes. We take in oxidant and fuel, we change the form of it, things move through membranes, and we oxygenate our blood - that's how nature works.

Neural connections, shown as the functional layers in figure 4.1, are formed in the brain at very early times in development, and at first they are present in an immature pattern of wiring that only grossly approximates the adult precision. In order for the adult pattern of connections to form, neural function is necessary. The adult brain consists of about 1 trillion (1012)-nerve cells, each connected to at least 20,000 other cells.

The possible combinations are greater than the number of molecules in the known universe. Each neuron makes a very stereotyped set of connections with specific partner neurons. Unlike common belief that our mind works like a computer, a useful analogy is to think of nerve cells as rather like a telephone system. Our brains employ a mixture of chemical and electrical signals to send and receive phone calls within the brain. Each nerve cell sends a long process, an axon-like a phone line- to connect itself to other cells that can be located the equivalent of hundreds of miles away. The brain contains well over 1,000 trillion connections.

Learning

Learning can be defined as the process of connectivity of the nodes within your neural network of the brain. The mind is like the stomach. It's not how much you put into it, but how much it digests. Knowledge is the only instrument of production that is not subject to diminishing returns.

During brain connectivity development (i.e., education), all these connections have to be formed from scratch-nerve cells are made in different places in the brain by undergoing many successive cell divisions. Then each cell has to spin out its long process towards the appropriate target neurons.

The process is much like stringing phone lines from one city to another, for instance. First, trunk lines between the two cities must be laid down. Then, phones at specific addresses within each city need to be wired so that when a specific phone number is dialed, only that phone rings and not the wrong numbers.

The brain first sets down a basic framework of circuits-rather like trunk lines according to strict circuit diagrams determined by a genetic blueprint. Then, long before the adult precise circuits are formed, the "switch" is turned on: brain function itself completes the wiring process by running test patterns on the circuits, thereby selecting correct connections and eliminating errors.

Using the phone analogy, it is as if, once the trunk lines are strung between two cities, the first set of phone calls to be placed cause many phones to ring because many connections, including the correct ones, are formed initially. Then, a process of error-correction occurs, in which phoning it eliminates the incorrect connections and strengthens the correct ones. Special early cell types in the brain place these molecules in specific combinations and locations, and they are sensed molecularly by the growing axon tips of "pioneer" neurons as they spin out the first connections.

Once these early connections are formed, neural function begins and neurons signal to each other by sending chemical-electrical signals over their long distance connections. In the phoning process itself, the frequent use of connections strengthens them with rewards of special nerve growth factors and other signalling molecules. The inappropriate use of wrong connections causes their elimination. It is in this second phase of wiring where experience of the world can have a profound influence on the selection and maintenance of connections.

This observation forms the basis for the classic model of the critical period for brain development. Because different parts of the brain mature at different rates and times, neuroscientists believe there are different critical periods for different functions. A challenge for the future is to learn exactly what those periods are in terms of the specific development of brain circuits, for instance, for language acquisition, or reading.

An initial activity-independent step in which the basic framework of connections is constructed strictly according to the genetic blueprint, followed by a step in which brain function selects and refines from a wealth of possible connections. This second step is a prolonged period that experience can profoundly influence the important details of brain circuitry.

There are just not enough genes to account for the incredible precision of connectivity present in the adult brains. An elegant solution is to "hard wire" the trunk lines with specific molecular guidance clues, but then flip the switch to "on" early and let neural function make the final decisions. And this flexibility in final decision-making, after all, is what lets us adapt to our environment. For example, the brain does not know if it is going to have to learn English, Spanish, or Japanese after birth.

An elegant solution to the wiring problem is to establish the fundamental framework of language circuitry using strict molecular mechanisms and then sculpt out the details depending on specific experiences after birth. Without this superb flexibility, we could not learn or remember or adapt to our environment-in short, those properties that make us uniquely human. Not much useful theory has been developed to explain how "reason for decision" and "cause for action" are related. A primary reason for this lack of knowledge is that reason for decision is treated as a multi-faceted and rich construct, while cause for action is an external manifestation which is subject to interpretation.

Categorisation process: Categorisation is the cognitive process by which distinct entities are treated as equivalent. It allows us to understand and make predictions about objects and events in our world. The categorisation process is based on criteria to group together entities in the same category. These criteria include perceptual or structural similarity, and the commonalties of their elements that provide homogeneity about the entities that belong to them.

The categorisation of objects and concepts facilitate a common goal and serve the similar function. As we deepen our understanding of the external world, the representation of concepts and objects changes. Therefore, the categorisation process is intimately tied to our new criteria, and the context in which the entities influence the way they are classified.

Persistence of a model: Mind retains a thought process of a model of an external world for limited duration, unless a new thought replaces it. For example, when someone is talking to you, his/her voice echos in your mind, till you replace it with new thought. It is evident that the mind retains vision for a split second. This accounts for the fact that when a motion picture flashes a series of progressive images, instead of the mind seeing the flashing of a series of images, it sees the illusion of motion.

Motivation in making decisions: The mind is generally unwilling to allocate energy to decisions whose value it is not convinced. The unspoken and even unconscious questions "what is it good for?" and "will I be able to do that?" can frequently stymie our efforts to take in a decision.

Information versus knowledge: Information is a commodity capable of yielding knowledge. Knowledge is information-produced by self. Information possesses a meaning which can only be interpreted in the light of knowledge. Purposeful action is based, not on information, but on knowledge. There are two types of knowledge: knowing that, and know how. We all know that 12X12 = 144. "Knowing how" is more critical since it captures "knowledge about" rather than "knowledge of" which belongs to memory.

"Knowing how" requires systematic study and reflection, judgement, proposition, testing, and its integration with some other relevant forms of know-how. "Knowing how" is an ultimate source of strategic advantage within the organisational systems of the firm. Simply knowing how is not enough, because there might be other ways of achieving the same goal. For example, Nissan's plants in Japan, Mexico and the US use different mixes of technology and labour to create the same cars with almost similar overall productivity.

Knowledge base which is a set of facts and rules obtained from experience and stored in our memory. Knowledge isn't how much you have committed to memory. It's being able to differentiate between what you do know and what you don't. It's the correct connectivity of the brain neural networks and how wide these networks are. As we age, we use different parts of the brain for memory tasks.

Recent studies have found that older adults use their frontal cortex for simple short-term memory tasks. Younger people use that area for complex short-term memory tasks. Older adults also activate both hemispheres for spatial memory; younger people use the left hemisphere. Inference is a part of neural network of our brains that analyses available data and the facts and rules stored in the knowledge base of the brain.

Understanding is the integrated mind that is able to span the relevant functional areas across the brain by the neural network connectivity. What is it indeed that gives us the feeling of elegance in understanding? It is the harmony of the diverse parts, their symmetry, their happy balance; in a word it is all that introduces order, all that gives unity, that permits us to see clearly and to comprehend at once both the ensemble and the details.

Non-sensory experiences represent almost all context information in consciousness. They condition most aspects of conscious cognition including voluntary retrieval, perception, monitoring, problem solving, emotion, and evaluation, meaning recognition. Many peculiar aspects of non-sensory qualitative context that resist being 'grasped' by an act of attention, are explained as adaptations shaped by the cognitive functions they serve.

The most important non-sensory experience is coherence or "rightness." Rightness represents degrees of context fit among contents in consciousness, and between conscious and non-conscious processes. Rightness is the feeling-of-knowing in implicit cognition. The experience of rightness suggests that neural mechanisms "compute" signals indicating the global dynamics of the neural network integration.

Understanding is the ability to give meaning. In other words, understanding is possible only by an anticipation of meaning which it constitutes interconnectivity of a specific and limited neural networks. The interconnectivity exhausts itself to a resourceful finite thought called understanding. This implies that, if it takes a lot of words to say what you have in mind, give it more thought.

Consecutive strategic thinking is a process which does not allow you to go out of the boundary of the subject of your thought. This focusing process should be taught at an early education. For example, a student in the class can be called upon to talk for five minutes about his/her uncle, when he/she goes out of the boundary and talks about uncles' neighbour for too long the class will shout "you are out of focus".

Focusing on one-thing-at-a-time: The prefrontal cortex and other key areas of the brain handle tasks like a browser. When doing two things, those parts of the brain repeatedly switch from one task to another. Therefore, it's better to do one thing at a time rather than three things at once. Otherwise, your lost time when moving from one task to another increases even more with the complexity of the problem. Since activating the rules for each task takes several tenths of a second, therefore multitasking, in the end, takes more time than doing one thing at a time.

Why do we need to analyse? We need analysis because our minds think about specific and limited ways, one thing at a time. Then, after the analysis process, we synthesise what belongs together to see the whole or to solve the problem. There are different moods of knowledge such as: symbolic knowledge, declarative knowledge, representation, and procedural knowledge. For example, symbolic knowledge is needed for development of mathematical and statistical thinking.

Experiences and feelings are inherently conscious states. There is something it is like to feel pain, to have an itch, to experience bright red. Philosophers call this sort of consciousness "phenomenal consciousness." Even though phenomenal consciousness seems to be a relatively primitive matter, something more widespread in nature than higher-order or reflective consciousness, it is deeply puzzling.

Why are people different? We are all different because we all have different history. Thoughts and emotions give us a sense of continuity, our identities, create our conscious selves, our personalities which are not "localised" components of the brain, but are a function of the organism's life-history, cumulative experience, the totality of memories stored, recollected, analysed, modified, and retained in the physical configurations of the network-connectivity in the brain.

Experience includes the collection of all the mistakes we have made in the past. Recently, a manager was asked if he was going to fire an employee who made a mistake that cost the company Rs.600,000. No, the manager replied, "I just spent Rs.600,000 training him. Why would I want somebody to hire his experience."

Roots of decision-making

The West was born 500 years ago when Europe broke free of the centralised control of the Roman Catholic Church. Self and consciousness has diverse perspectives, including, Psychology, Sociology, Philosophy, Neuroscience, Cognitive Science, and Media Studies, etc. The active topics relevant to decision-making in these areas are:

1. *Where we came from:* Self and consciousness in pre-human species. Are humans really unique? and through human history is there something special about modern self and consciousness?
2. *Where we are now:* Humans as biological beasts and cognitive creatures — The brain and mind as biological and cognitive systems underlying self and consciousness.
3. *Where we are now:* Humans as social beings — The social underpinnings of self and consciousness, including how self and consciousness emerge in face-to-face interactions over the course of development and how societal belief systems impact and often disturb the self and consciousness of individuals.
4. *Where we might go:* Where humans will likely go in the future, including how human selves and consciousness might be changed by interacting with computers and related electronic media.

Perception of colour, sounds and their physical reality: We see colours for a purpose and the act of seeing is part of what the later Wittgenstein called a language game. For instance, a good apple is an edible colour, so it is wrong to reduce colours to waves, as their function is much wider.

The same applies to sounds and airwaves; the growl of a bear is not really airwaves in the wider context of danger. Because they serve a functional purpose, sensible images cannot be reduced to isolated scientific facts but exist in their own right as primaries. Their perception is usually right because of evolution, whether we consider colours as wavelengths, or photon's states energy. The brain's perceived image and sound are a construct put together according to what we "expect" to see or hear.

Deciding among models: Suppose you decide to use a model for a particular process for making concrete decisions about your own life and those of others, who may be affected, directly or indirectly, by your decisions, that is the ultimate reason why we have models? We create some models de novo from our own experience, but most we learn from external sources, including formal education.

Now, supposing one is presented with two apparently competing models of a process. One of them has more objective evidence for its validity in the form of scientifically controlled studies, ability to be mathematically confirmed, reliable historical documentation, endorsement by experts in the field, and so forth. The other is untested and perhaps un-testable, and is endorsed by people with less impressive pedigrees. However, based on your limited experience, applying model B in cases where the two differ in their recommendations produces a better result.

RUMOUR, BELIEF, OPINION, AND FACT

As a necessity the human rational strategic thinking has evolved to cope with his/her environment. The rational strategic thinking which we call reasoning is another means to make the world calculable, predictable, and more manageable for the utilitarian purposes. In constructing a model of reality, factual information is therefore needed to initiate any rational strategic thinking in the form of reasoning. However, we should not confuse facts with beliefs, opinions, or rumours.

Beliefs are defined as someone's own understanding. In belief, "I am" always right and "you" are wrong. There is nothing that can be done to convince the person that what they believe is wrong. With respect to belief, Henri Poincaré said, "Doubt everything or believe everything: these are two equally convenient strategies. With either, we dispense with the need to think." Believing means not wanting to know what is fact.

Human beings are most apt to believe what they least understand. Therefore, you may rather have a mind opened by wonder than one closed by belief. The greatest derangement of the mind is to believe in something because one wishes it to be so. Religion is the most widely debated and least agreed upon phenomenon of human history. The history of humanity is filled with unsettling normative perspectives reflected in, for example, inquisitions, witch hunts, denunciations, and brainwashing techniques.

The "sacred beliefs" are not only within religion, but also within ideologies, and could even include science. In much the same way that Thomas Kuhn observed that scientists trying to "save the theory." For example, the Freudian treatment is a kind of brainwashing by the therapist where the patient is in a suggestive mood completely and religiously believing in whatever the therapist is making of him/her and blaming himself/herself in all cases.

The use of religion, psychoanalysis, or the mass media, as instruments by which people are helped to adjust to a dehumanising social order without being challenged to change it, is essentially a betrayal of man. There is this huge lumbering momentum from the Cold War where thinking is still not appreciated. Nothing is so firmly believed as that which is least known. For example, many people do not believe the official spokesman from the government, however, they trust "an unidentified source".

The fact of the matter is that there is no hip world and there is no straight world. There's a world, you see, which has people in it that believes in a variety of different things. Everybody believes in something and everybody, by virtue of the fact that they believe in something, uses that something to support their own existence.

Whoever believes in something will have an ever lasting-life. The cultural history is littered with discarded belief-models. However, this does not mean that someone who didn't understand what was going on invented the model nor had no utility or practical value. The main idea was the cultural values of any wrong model. The falseness of a belief is not necessarily an objection to a belief. The question is, to what extent is it life-promoting, and life enhancing for the believer? As an example, to attain happiness in another world we need only to believe something, while to secure it in this world we must make good decisions.

The natural right authorises a person to do to others anything that does not in itself diminish what is theirs, so long as they do not want to accept it—such things as merely communicating his thoughts to them, telling or promising them something, whether what he says is true and sincere or untrue and insincere; for it is entirely up to them whether they want to believe him or not. As Stoic philosophy teaches us: It is beyond our control whether others choose to insult us or offend us in some way, but it is always in our control whether we choose to be insulted or offended. If we want to remain eudaimon and tranquil, it would be wise not to be easily insulted or offended.

Opinions (or feelings) are slightly less extreme than beliefs, however, they are dogmatic. An opinion means that a person has certain views that they think are right. Also, they know that others are entitled to their own opinions. People respect others' opinions and in turn expect the same. In forming one's opinion, the empirical observations are obviously strongly affected by attitude and perception. However, opinions that are well rooted should grow and change like a healthy tree.

Fact is the only instructional material that can be presented in an entirely non-dogmatic way. Everyone has a right to his/her own opinion, but no one has a right to be wrong in his/her facts. Opinions have vested interests just as everyone has. Public opinion is often a sort of religion, with the majority as its prophet. Moreover, the prophet has a short memory and does not provide consistent opinions over time.

An opinion, right or wrong can never constitute an offense, nor in itself an obligation. It may be mistaken, involve an absurdity, or be a contradiction. It is a truth or it is an error but it can never be a crime, or a virtue. Rumours and gossip are even weaker than opinion. Now the question is who will believe these? For example, rumours and gossip about a person are those when you hear something you like, about someone you do not.

Here is an example you might be familiar with: Why is there no Nobel Prize for mathematics? It is the opinion of many that Alfred Nobel caught his wife in an amorous situation with Mittag-Leffler, the foremost Swedish mathematician at the time. Therefore, Nobel was afraid that if he were to establish a mathematics prize, the first to get it would be M-L. The story persists, no matter how often one repeats the plain fact that Nobel was not married.

It is curious how much more interest can be evoked by a mixture of gossip, belief, and opinion than by facts. To understand the difference between feeling and strategic thinking, consider carefully the following true statement: He that thinks himself the happiest man really is so; but he that thinks himself the wisest is generally the greatest fool. Most people do not ask for facts in making up their decisions. They would rather have one good, soul-satisfying emotion than a dozen facts. This does not mean that you should not feel anything. Notice your feelings. But do not think with them.

Facts are different than beliefs, rumours, and opinions. Facts are the basis of decisions. A fact is something that is right and one can prove to be true based on evidence and logical arguments. A fact can be used to convince yourself, your friends, and your enemies. Facts are always subject to change. Data becomes information when it becomes relevant to your decision problem.

Information becomes fact when the data can support it. Fact becomes knowledge when it is used in the successful completion of a structured decision process. However, a fact becomes an opinion if it allows for different interpretations, i.e., different perspectives. Note that what happened in the past is fact, not truth. Truth is what we think about, what happened (i.e., a model).

Science and religion are profoundly different. Religion asks us to believe without question, even (or especially) in the absence of hard evidence. Indeed, this is essential for having a faith. Science asks us to take nothing on faith, to be wary of our penchant for self-deception, to reject anecdotal evidence. Science considers deep but healthy skepticism a prime feature. One of the reasons for its success is that science has built-in, error-correcting machinery at its very heart.

Learn how to approach information critically and discriminate in a principled way between beliefs, opinions, and facts. Critical thinking is needed to produce well-reasoned representation of reality in your modelling process. Analytical thinking demands clarity, consistency, evidence, and above all, a consecutive, focused-thinking. Examples of belief, opinion, and facts can be found in religions, economics, and econophysics, respectively.

Management Science is built up with facts, as a house is with stones. But a collection of facts is no more a useful science for the manager than a heap of stones is a house. To meet the essence for communication, judgement, and persuasion of knowledge, your model must include, among others:

1. It must explain the phenomena of interest — which means, you must be able to derive or create the phenomena using the model.
2. It must predict future phenomena.
3. You must make a good case for ruling out alternative explanations.

For example, in order to rule out alternative explanations, you first need to know what your client would think of as plausible explanations (models). This means, you must get "subjective" with your clients and encourage them to provide their best shot at causal explanations before you build your model. And it means you also have to think very hard about what a harsh critic of your model will say — what alternative explanations they could use to discredit your efforts.

You score big if your model explains, and, even more dramatically, if it predicts, something that their formulations do not. You also score big if, with the deeper understanding provided by your model, it becomes evident that their explanation does not work.

Consciousness and the mind: Contrary to philosophical tradition, modern theorists of the mind have often downplayed the importance of consciousness. Instead, they have accounted for the mind in terms of phenomena like mechanisms, dispositions, abilities and even environmental features. One of many inspirations for this trend is that a variety of specific mental phenomena, like searching, comparing, understanding and reading are involved. These cases may exemplify any of the phenomena at issue without being in any particular type of conscious state however; consciousness may be a more important aspect of the mind than is supposed.

In order to understand consciousness one would benefit from developing a more eclectic intellectual style. Consciousness is, as proposed by almost everyone except the reductionists, a truly mysterious concept. Its study and dissection merits a multidisciplinary approach. Waving this multi-disciplinary flag has positively enlarged the discussion and neurologists, psychiatrists, mathematicians, and so on, have moved to the philosophy of mind arena, first with caution and now with a more powerful voice.

Identifying what we mean by consciousness is a first step and the link between consciousness and some other mental activity, e.g., awareness, memory, executive functioning, etc., is a logical step. Knowledge has four necessary conditions: It must be justifiable, It must be true, It must be believable, and It must rules out counter-examples.

5

COGNITIVE AND BEHAVIOURAL DECISION-MAKING

Decision-making is the central activity for both leaders and managers. Managing and leading are not the same. The manager's responsibility is "To Do the Things Right", and the leader's responsibility is "To Do the Right Things". Leaders have a goal of creating an innovative environment that will of necessity produce mistakes, and managers have a goal of honing their craft to reduce and eliminate mistakes and waste.

The assumption that cognition can be studied by looking exclusively at what goes on in the brain has undergone considerable criticism. A diverse and growing number of researchers claim that an organism's cognitive abilities are partly constituted by prior and posterior conception, action, environmental manipulation and intricate couplings that spread the causality across organisms and structures in their physical, social, and technological environments.

Research in this area is interdisciplinary in nature, drawing on fields such as philosophy, cognitive science, developmental studies, neuroscience, artificial intelligence, simulation science and robotics. Much of it is inspired by or complemented by the insights of thinkers in the phenomenological area that emphasize the ways in which experience and thought are structured by bodily constraints and environmental interaction.

COGNITIVE DECISION THEORY

This is an empirical, descriptive, non-statistical, context related process theory and considers a "decision" as a decision-making process very similar to a problem solving process, which is a special, time consuming context dependent information processing process. The human decision-maker is considered in analogy to a computer system, i.e. data and knowledge has to be fed into the system. This and the type of information processing performed determine the outcome.

Connectionist Paradigm

Neural nets also model living (human) information processing, but on a more physical and not so functional level. Information is processed from input via hidden to output layers of artificial neurons. One of the differences between the "cognitive" and the "neural" decision model is, that the latter includes explicitly and even concentrates on learning and on topological features, while the former does not exclude learning but does not consider it as one of the points of major interest.

The most important issue for the strategic decision-maker is the outcome of decisions. Clearly, what we think or feel is not relevant to the physical world, however they influence on the value judgment in the goal setting. The decision-maker's model is based one readily measurable — either from actual decisions or from surveys polls, or interactive simulations. Statistical techniques deal with the validity, applicability, and scalability of such information. This information can then be used to rigorously model the decisions as a function of perceived conditions and personal tastes, values, and preferences. Qualitative Choice Theory is one of the more popular approaches in that it is easily calibrated and parameterised, is robust, and has the feature that allows "analogous" decision data to be applied to new situations.

The OR/MS/DS/SS modelling process aims at structuring complex problems, exploring different perspectives and facilitating participation and engagement of the decision-maker with the OR/MS/DS/SS analyst. The success in OR/MS/DS/SS modelling requires both quantitative (hard) and qualitative (soft) data together in a single engagement. The real-world decision problems exist within a complex organisational context that has both social and personal dimensions. Moreover various stages of the OR/MS/DS/SS modelling process, from the initial stage of understanding the problem, to the final stage of implementing a good strategy, require a different and appropriate method and technique for a particular decision problem.

Unfortunately, the devolution of OR/MS/DS/SS has been from a concern with real-world problems to one with applications of mathematical techniques. Much published research in OR/MS/DS/SS is unengaged and focused on decision mathematics or optimisation. That is, most papers published in leading OR/MS/DS/SS journals take little or no account of how their finding might be used in practice, nor do they express much concern about this issue.

The management scientist is not the decision-maker. The decision-maker must incorporate other necessary perspectives including the organisational, environmental, conflicting, historical, political, dynamic, and psychological aspects of the problem into the management scientist's analytical model.

One must be cautioned that the way we choose to see the world (i.e., modelling) creates the world we see. When describing reality, you must be careful not to weave in your own wishful views. For example, describing nature as if it has human traits is a modelling process called the "pathetic fallacy." It has been found that, so far as we can discover, nature is indifferent to the values and can only be understood by ignoring the notions of good and bad. The Universe may have a purpose, but nothing we know suggests that this purpose has any similarity to ours.

The Pythagorean' view of the world was to study the world as an external entity. This gave rise to the Western scientific and analytical tradition. However, the mysticism view of Eastern world, as expressed, is based on the attitude that man is inseparable from the world.

We deplete nature's natural resources by using or even abusing them up to their limits. This reality must constantly remind us that there is a place for man somewhere between these extreme views. In abusing nature, Wally Hickel, a former governor of Alaska, defended and justified his decisions by believing that "you can't just let nature run wild." Sustainability requires living within the regenerative capacity of the biosphere. However, human demands have already exceeded the biosphere's regenerative capacity.

Man can be Programmed

Anyone who has read Etienne de la Boetie, Margaret Mead, or John Dewey will recognise that we are all programmed by our cultures. We accept as unfailing truisms that are not really truths but leading us into folly. The "Dominator Paradigm" recognised the dominants and domineering world view by the power of the sword (Arm force), the flag (Nationalism), and the cross (Religion).

The procedure for domination invariably followed the three steps:

1. Learn the dominant myths of the target people and, in the process, gain their trust.
2. Find the gaps or superstitions in their beliefs.
3. Either replace the superstitions or augment them with facts that redirect the target group's perceptions and allegiance.

The programme started with the Jewish Creation Myth that the universe was created for man. The Greeks extended the concept with the dictum that "man is the measure of all things." The Inquisition made heresy to think otherwise and burned over a million witches at the stake (mostly beautiful young women) to impress it on society. Columbus started the spread of the Dominator Paradigm world wide during the age of "discovery" and colonisation.

Adam Smith started the trend to make it the ethical base of the Euro-American culture with his concept that by "self-interest" and an "unseen hand" economics would solve all of the social and ethical problems. USA has achieved its commercial and financial supremacy under a regime of private ownership. It conquered the wilderness, built our railroads, our factories, our public utilities, gave us the telegraph, the telephone, the electric light, the automobile, the airplane, the radio and a higher standard of living for all the people than obtains anywhere else in the world. Not many great inventions ever came from a government-owned industry.

As Friedrich Nietzsche has said, "The task is to rediscover beneath all flattering colours and make-up the frightful prototext homo natura, which means to translate man back into nature; to become master over the many vain and overlay enthusiastic interpretations and connotations that have so far been scrawled and painted over that eternal basic text of homo natura." At the basis of the whole modern view of the world lies the illusion that the so-called laws of nature are the interpretations of natural phenomena. This does not take a law-giver into discount.

Any general statements such as "everyone will have some kind of middle life crisis, such as depression, during their middle-age or at a later stage in his/her life time" may not be correct. Humans have no nature to be discovered, but they do have history. It was necessary for humans to abandon all instincts to become a member of society by following its norms and customs. It is impossible to overlook the extent to which civilisation is built upon a renunciation of instinct. Almost nothing is left in humans to be called instinct, common sense, or other similar names.

Social Cognitive

Social Cognitive (SC) is the property of a systems whereby the collective behaviours of entities interacting locally with their environment cause coherent functional global patterns to emerge. SC provides a basis with which it is possible to explore collective and distributed decision-making without centralised control or the provision of a global model. To tackle the formation of a coherent social collective intelligence from individual behaviours, it must consider concepts related to self-organisation, and the social bounds. It also includes the role played not only by the environmental media as a driving force for societal learning, but also by positive and negative feedback produced by the interactions among agents. The results will be the collective adaptation of a social community to its dynamic cultural environment.

Intuition is a Mode of Fast Thinking

Intuitive state is a rapid selective cycling and recycling gathering information and ideas from one's memory and applying value to them. This is done so fast that one cannot have a clear record of what is happening. Intuition may not always help you in finding the right answer to even a simple question. Suppose you are filling two ice cube trays with water, boiling hot in one, cold in the other, and placing both in a freezer. The question is: Which tray turns to ice quicker?" If your answer is the tray with boiling hot water, then you are right. Why? How could you resolve this apparent isolation of the laws of thermodynamics.

Why do different managers make different decisions for a given problem? Why are we all different? Because we all have different experiences and unique backgrounds. Every experience in life shapes our mind in a unique way. Knowledge is a biological phenomenon. Humans experience the world in their own ways. Through their internal processes, each human engages in a creative relationship with the external world, bringing forth a myriad of different models. The history of science shows how weak common sense, instinct, and intuition can be taken as guides to our understanding.

Use of Models

A model is not a property of the reality, but of its description. Models are useful but they all certainly come with their own baggage of simplification, and theorisation of reality, however, the price for not modelling is eternal obfuscation. A model could be as good as "virtual reality", however, it is never the "real reality." Unfortunately, in many cases, modelling becomes an end rather than a means. The modeller spends so much time in creating the model that he/she falls in love with the model: the model becomes the reality. Do not take a "model" as the "reality." Unfortunately, many do. There are much more models in the world than realities. For a successful decision, reality must take precedence over the decision model, for reality cannot be fooled.

Effective Communication Skills

The management scientist must know that his/her success depends on effective communication skills (i.e., making common what is individually experienced). Proper focus on communicating the results and recommended course of action obtained by the modeller is needed. This helps to achieve a consensus concerning an acceptable course of action. Finally, be aware that in many historical cases humans invented some models of reality in order to discard the reality itself.

HUMAN PERFORMANCE TECHNOLOGY

Human performance is the key to unlocking markets and organisations. New technologies open many options for what we do and how and where we do it. They allow new processes, new structures, new strategies. But the good decision-makers will build their plans on a simple platform. Human performance is at the core of business performance. They will put the human issues front and centre of their strategies and their execution plans, and they will bring rigour, discipline, and mathematical modelling to match the way they develop and apply technology.

Qualitative considerations such as re-organisation and refinements are as important as quantitative factors in an effective strategic decision-making process. The main question is How to merge different mental models within an organisation a shared mental model? The progression in that direction might be one of the following two possibilities:

1. If the organisation contains conflicting mental models it will not move far, resulting in political infighting.
2. If the organisation contains a single mental model (i.e., consensus) it can move in that direction until it comes up against the reality when it requires an adaptation.

Over time, however, the organisation whose mental models most closely match the reality will survive, while others fail.

Cognitive decision science: The cognitive decision science concerns the nature of the decision-maker intentions. Often intentions are entities of thinking, which are introspectively accessible to the conscious mind, and causally efficacious in the production of implementation of the decision, i.e., intentional realism of the decision. However, intentions might be conceived of as abstract patterns discernable in the behaviour of organisms, which are ascribed as instruments of prediction, without much awareness of internal representational machinery responsible for the implantation of the decisions.

The third model of cognitive decision science rightly considers both processes: the choices and the subjectivity of re-evaluation of all values as the measure of intentional and the final decision.

Cognitive impairments factors: The following factors may impair the decision-making process performance including speed, reasoning, planning, judgement, impulse control, temper control, perception, awareness, attention, language, learning, memory and timing.

Disorganisation: Difficulties in planning, organisation, sequencing and prioritising.

Lack of initiation: The initiation or starting of an activity, conversation or behaviour is often compromised.

Fixed mindedness: Perseverance or being fixed on a specific thought or action can occur when behaviours are inadequately regulated by the brain.

Impulsivity: Some persons experience difficulties with impulse control and may develop problem behaviours such as irritability, temper outbursts, and acting without thinking

BEHAVIOURAL DECISION-MAKING

Physical sciences are in general based on the cause-and-effect logic. Human's behaviours are, however based on motives. There is always a motivation force generated by some causes and purposes that can tell why a person makes a particular decision, i.e., the Emotivisim School of thought.

Managers wish to motivate workers to exert effort. For example, there is large literature on the use of wages and monetary incentives for this purpose, but in practice the "honour" or "prestige" of an award can be a significant motivator as well, unless the award is given so often that its prestige is diluted.

The main focus must be on management of the reputation of an award that may or may not have a fixed monetary component but how to manage the award over time.

The cardinal aim of modelling human behaviour is to model a business process that increases workforce enthusiasm considering all aspects of human behaviour including group dynamics, project work climate, and organisational culture.

Classification of Behavioural Decision-Making

Decision-making types may allows for only three unique systems of making decisions:

1. *Individualism*—which access inequity, relishes competition and identifies with the rights and power of the individual.
2. *Collaboration*—which treats all men as equally important, exalts collaborative efforts and identifies with unlimited democracy.
3. *Power and authority*—which respects power and identifies with controlling authority.

An organisational system based upon the "nature of man" blends the three possible systems into a harmonious unity, accepting that any one of the systems standing alone is both unstable and ineffective.

The universality of the three decision-making processes seems obvious. Everyone wants to be free to make his or her own decisions. At the same time, everyone needs the companionship and the sense of belonging that comes with being part of a group, and everyone fears the absolute solitude of unrestricted freedom. Finally, everyone wants to believe in something or someone, to conform his or her behaviour to some kind of authority, whether that authority comes internally from religious, political, or cultural values or externally from a leader in a hierarchy.

While it may seem obvious that everyone relies upon these three types of decision-making, the political conversations often polarise into conflicts of two decision-making types, a battle of group consensus versus individual freedom. We have dogmas of the "left" and "right" or of "liberals" and "conservatives." Conforming to these dogmas is a serious blunder. Dogmas of the left or right fail to recognise the role that authority plays in balancing the interests of the group and the individual. Without a balance of all three types, organisations can quickly become unstable and ineffective.

Organisations use decision-making processes that vary from elaborate designs with numerous decision points to relatively simple procedures. In each case, the process relies on a mix of the three types of decision-making inherent in human thinking:

1. Individual decision-making based upon self interest,
2. Group decision-making based upon consensus, and
3. Authoritative decision-making based upon values, rules and hierarchies. The organisations that succeed during both good times and bad times are those that maintain an effective balance between these three ways of choosing a course of action. In fact, what we regard as a "civil" society is one that balances the three decision-making methods in a constant tug of war. As a result, modern "civil" societies facilitate the creation of balanced organisations.

There have been two extreme approaches to modelling human behaviour. The simple models emphasis on "rational persons," while other's emphasis is on the fact that people have much more complex motivations, both individually and collectively, especially in herd-instinct, or malicious-intent situations.

An integrative descriptive model for human behaviour must consider all aspects of decision-making factors including use the economic, sociology, law, and social psychology. This might be achieved at three levels: the individual, the organisation, and the society, with interactions among the three. The interactions among these three levels include flows of information, and resources, and within each system of values and decision structures. These two kinds of flows shape the interactions between these three levels.

Good Decision and Unfavourable Outcome

Often an unfavourable outcome of a good decision leads individuals to switch away from that decision due to negative emotional responses to the outcome. Negative emotional reactions led many to abandon the option that they recalled as having been more successful in the past and which they expected to perform better in the future. They focus on their affective reactions rather than beliefs about the earlier disappointing outcome. Those individuals with a general tendency to focus on their needed cognition are less likely to switch away from the better option following a disappointing outcome. It is also likely that an emotional reaction to a negative outcome lead people to switch away from the options that they believe might be successful on the next occasion.

Feeling versus being: Feeling is different form being. Feeling is the mind response while being is the bodily manifestation of the same thing. For example, feeling of being sad is an emotion, which is not measurable, however, being sad, is a bodily response and therefore, the degree of being sadness is measurable on numerical scales by the appropriate psychometric instruments.

Conflict is a Part of Life

People and businesses suffer when conflict is ignored and not managed properly. Relationships are strained, productivity diminishes, and destruction can be the ultimate result. Many of us are so averse to conflict that we practice appeasement at any price, while others cling to adversarial approaches, which can escalate all the costs of settling differences. These behaviours are often the spawning ground for further conflict. They occur because we do not know about how to effectively use the array of possibilities that exist for successful conflict management. The OR/MS/DS/SS use of conflict modelling is in model-based decision support systems, i.e., the use of flexible, user-friendly software to build up systems of decision-makers, set of options, and preferences. This facilitates rapid change in one's assumptions, and conditions among the participants.

Behavioural decision-making is to understand how people make decisions and how they can make the decision-making process more effective and efficient. A person could be very conservative, or perpetual in making any decision. The behaviour sciences are applicable to decision processes from both quantitative and qualitative viewpoints to improve a stronger foundation for making better decisions. The decision-maker's style and characteristics can be classified as: the thinker, the cowboy (snap and uncompromising), Machiavellian (ends justifies the means), the historian (how others did it), the cautious (even nervous), etc.

Habits and Decision-Making

Decision-making involves reaching a conclusion, which implies deliberation and thought and suggests a conscious act. While a natural reaction or unconscious act would be labelled as habit, reflex act, or impulsive act, or habit which is, unfortunately the center of gravity when we want to start the decision-making process.

Power and the Leadership

Strategy implementation is a political process that involves bargaining, persuasion, and confrontation among actors who divide power.

People in power usually want to stay there. And one way they think they can do this is by enforcing rigid adherence to a set of principles that they believe are responsible for their organisation's success. By requiring employees to abide by these superstitions — better known as company policies — rather than examining the facts, they build organisations that appear streamlined. In fact, they are doomed.

There is no such thing as "organisational behaviour;" it is the behaviour of the people in the organisation. It is impossible to understand the decision-maker's behaviour in organisational situations where conflict exists without considering the role of power. Power has a major impact on information, uncertainty, and resource dependency since there is competition among organisation's members for scarce resources. There is a big difference between management and leadership: while management works in the system, leadership works on the system. If one is able enough to accurately define all three of these parameters; Task, Time, and Resources, then one is able to deal with the decision-making modelling process. The very essence of leadership is that you have to have vision for these parameters. You can't blow an uncertain trumpet.

Leadership is defined as, "the quality of a leader, and the capacity to lead." It can also be defined as setting the example. Whether they realise it or not, a given staff will look to the leader to set the trend in the workplace. So what trend are you setting? There is a reason the CEO of a multi-billion dollar international soft drink company spends one day a month delivering cases of soda via delivery truck and wheeled dolly. Because he's smart and successful, and his staff is watching him like a hawk. They can't help but copy and respect the CEO's sense of enthusiasm and commitment to what the business is really all about—getting product into customer's hands.

The challenge of leadership is mainly its human-side. The leader is to be strong, but not rude; kind, but not weak; bold, but not a bully; thoughtful, but not lazy; humble, but not timid; proud, but not arrogant; and have a sense of humour, without folly. Before the leaders can inspire with emotion, they must be swamped with it themselves. Before they can move the tears of others, their own must flow. To convince others, they must themselves believe.

Unethical and Evil Decisions

One must certainly be aware of the big difference between unethical and evil decisions. The CEO for an internationally known tire company signs off on the production of tires that he knows are likely to disintegrate under certain conditions. Even with such knowledge, he makes it clear that this information is not to be publicised and approves production and sales of the tires. Decide whether such a decision is an evil or unethical one? What about this scenario? An administrator in a fascist country followed the orders of his superior and signed off on the death of thousands of innocent men, women and children. He never personally killed any of those people himself nor would he. Without integrity, no company can have positive word of mouth.

The critical and postmodern organisation theorists have already built their case against Reason. They see reason as "disciplinary knowledge" in modern organisations because it constrains the natural autonomy of the individual. This view, all of the social sciences are seen as knowledge structures used in domination. Sociology, social work, law, psychology, and most certainly management and organisation theory are implicated. Just as psychology is used to persuade the individual to adjust to (thus accept) the external world, theories of leadership and organisation are used to develop discourses and classification schemes that reproduce systems of power. By rejecting Western cultural history, positioning the "naturalness" of the individual, and assuming all discipline is oppressive power generated by knowledge, critical organisation theory and postmodern organisation theory elevate individualism, although only implicitly, to the role of their supreme value.

Instrumental reasoning has been used successfully in science to make our world manageable. For its utilitarian characteristic, the instrumental reasoning is the supreme judge in any scientific field. It is possible to use reason to describe everything scientifically, but it would make no sense; it would be without meaning, as if you described a Beethoven ninth symphony as a variation of wave pressure.

Dealing with People

While senior management formulate clear strategies to achieve the essential fit between internal strengths and weaknesses and external threats and opportunities. However, strategy implementation is a social process rooted in culture, involving common interest and integration. People react and adapt to environmental changes and constraints.

There are two ways to persuade people. The first is by using conventional rhetoric, which is what most managers are trained in. The other way to persuade people and ultimately a much more powerful way is by uniting an idea with an emotional appeal.

In any organisation, it is a must for everyone to learn the ability to work with other people. Henry Ford used to say:

1. Coming together is a beginning;
2. Keeping together is progress;
3. Working together is success.

There are two different types of relationships among people namely the Frequent and Infrequent relationships. Negotiation is an effective tool for dealing with infrequent relationships. To have an effective negotiation one must separate the people from the problem, focus on interest (not taking positions), generate a variety of possibilities, and insist that the results be based on some objective numerable and measurable scales. For the ongoing relationships the strategies vary. The classical tactics are: carrots and sticks, tit-for-tat, and live-and-let-live.

Human abuse does not stem from a wanton exercise of power, rather, hurting people is a sign that we are still lacking power. Or it shows a sense of frustration in the face of this poverty. The blockage of self-developments is what lie behind abusive behaviour. Since whoever is dissatisfied with himself is continually ready for revenge and we others will be his victims. An eye for an eye will make the whole world go blind.

6

ROLE OF INTUITION IN DECISION-MAKING

Decision-making situations where intuitive approach can help most include the following.

1. Expedient decision-making and rapid response are required. The circumstances leave you no time to go through complete rational analysis.
2. Fast paced change. The factors on which you base your analysis change rapidly.
3. The problem is poorly structured.
4. The factors and rules that you need to take into account are hard to articulate in an unambiguous way.
5. You have to deal with ambiguous, incomplete, or conflicting information.
6. There is no precedent.

INTUITION

First, what do we mean by intuition in the context of decision-making? While different definitions emphasise different aspects, there are three key features that characterise the intuitive mode of thinking. The process is dominated by your subconscious mind, even if you use your conscious mind to formulate or rationalise the final results. The information is processed in parallel rather than sequentially. Instead of going through a logical sequence of thoughts one by one, you see the situation more as a whole, with different fragments emerging in parallel.

Intuition and Rational Analysis

The main alternative to the intuition-based approach is rational thinking. The rational decision-making process relies mostly on logic and quantitative analysis. You consciously analyse all the options. You formulate the main criteria for judging the expected outcomes of your options and you assign certain weights to those criteria to reflect their relative importance. Then, based on the expected outcomes and their weights, you rate your options by their perceived utility. Finally, you choose the option that has the highest rating.

If, for some options, the expected outcomes involve uncertainty, you will also need to incorporate in your ratings the perceived probabilities of different possibilities, or even perform a Monte Carlo simulation. Rational analysis still plays crucial role in many situations, especially when you have clear criteria and have to deal with extensive quantitative data, like quantitative finance. Yet, you will likely face even more business situations where the rational decision-making becomes impractical.

The simplest way to make sense of why and how intuition works is to think of it as an advanced pattern recognition device. Your subconscious mind somehow finds links between your new situation and various patterns of your past experiences. You may not recall most of the details of those experiences. And even if you did, it may be very hard to express the lessons you learnt in a form acceptable for analytical reasoning. Yet, your subconscious mind still remembers the patterns learnt. It can rapidly project your new circumstances onto those patterns and send you a message of wisdom. That message comes as your inner voice and will most likely be expressed in the language of your feelings.

USE OF INTUITIONS

The first important thing to keep in mind is that even when you rely on intuition it is still very important to do your homework. The intuition will help you navigate faster through much of unstructured data and can work around certain gaps and conflicts in the available information. Yet, even intuition can be misled if too many of your facts are wrong or missing.

Pay attention to your emotional state. If you are stressed or in a bad mood, your true inner voice will be distorted or lost in the background of your strong negative feelings. A similar effect may happen with strong positive feelings. If you want to hear your inner voice, get over the background of your strong feelings. Feel them through or let them go. Take a walk. Do something refreshing. Say your prayers. Forgive and accept. Sigh. Unclutter your mind.

Finally, you can greatly increase the quality of your intuitive decisions if you include certain elements of the analytical approach. In particular, try to follow the procedure of the rational analysis first. As much as you can, capture on paper the ideas on the main options and the criteria for evaluating your choices. Write down the key facts and factors you need to keep in mind.

Following this procedure is an effective way to feed your subconscious mind with all the relevant data it needs. You will help yourself even more if you put all those notes together on paper as a mind map. By having all the important points written in one place you will also unclutter your mind. At that stage you are much more ready to listen to your inner voice.

Mind Mapping Techniques

Mind mapping is a powerful technique for thinking on paper. It can help you greatly in such tasks as;

1. goal setting (goal mind mapping),
2. project planning,
3. organising information for decision-making,
4. studying new subjects or preparing for an exam,
5. preparing an oral presentation,
6. note taking,
7. brainstorming,
8. and many other "think on paper" types of situations.

Special role in the development and popularisation of mind mapping techniques for unleashing mind powers belongs to Tony Buzan, who is one of the leading authorities on learning techniques.

The rationale for the use of mind maps or concept maps comes from a deeper understanding of how the brain works with information. Unlike a traditional computer, your brain does not process or organise information in linear sequences.

Instead it naturally operates with networks of associations between various ideas. If you present information as a visual network, rather than a linear list, you will greatly enhance you mind powers to digest that information. You will also stimulate synergy of the left and right sides of your brain.

To create a concept map you can proceed in the following way. Take a sheet of paper and put in the middle the central concept of your topic of focus. For example, in the case of goal setting it can be the overall direction of your goals. Ideally, represent that concept as a combination of words and an image. Then, starting from that central concept, draw lines to the sides to represent the main related sub categories for your mind map topic.

Take one main keyword that you associate with each sub topic and print it in capitals over one of those lines. When you are done with those sub categories, continue the process of branching out lower level sub concepts. Draw lines from the end of each line from the previous stage and, as before, mark those lines with the main keywords that distinguish those concepts.

One variation of the technique is to put sub concepts as a network of bubbles connected with lines. The keywords are placed inside the bubbles rather than on the lines. You can enhance the visual power of your mind maps by putting images near some of the concepts. You can also benefit from using colours for better grouping of the related sub concepts.

In contrast to a linear list of text, a graphic concept map clearly represents relative importance of different sub concepts (by how far they are from the centre) as well as how much they are related to each other (by their proximity on paper). Mind map is also easier to extend than a continuous text. When you need to add a new concept, just find some space to branch out a new line.

While such visual exercise can be done on paper, there are also a few graphic mind mapping software tools that could streamline the process. Mind mapping software programmes greatly simplify visual map creation as well as management, especially when you need to modify, store, and organise your mind maps on a regular basis.

CLASSICAL MODEL OF DECISION-MAKING

The classical model of decision-making, which underlines the designing of MIS, is part of the rationalist tradition, which, since Plato, has considered cognition as a deliberative, analytic, deductive process.

In this viewpoint, cognition, in whatever form it takes—problem-solving, decision-making, learning, memorising-, involves manipulating symbols representing the characteristics of the world, according to certain logical rules; with, as a backdrop, the representation of the goal to be reached.

Making a decision would consist of breaking the original situation down into elementary facts represented by certain information, then applying logical rules to this information in order to obtain the set of possible plans of action, and finally evaluating the different alternatives which make it possible to reach the fixed objective.

In this way the manager would elaborate a clear, rational, explicit strategy: through a systematic analysis of the competitors and the markets, of the strengths and weaknesses of the organisation, this analysis based on the formalised representation of the operating system of the organisation and of its environment supplied by the MIS. Does this abstract representation of decision-making reflect the real experience of managers involved in their world of familiar situations? It does not seem that decisions "en acte", as they are lived and not as they are conceptualised, can be described by a process which consists of drawing conclusions from facts and rules.

As Henry Mintzberg has shown, the most creative strategies do not generally result from a deliberate process consisting of drawing conclusions from an objective representation of the situation, but rather from a non-intentional mode of action; only the carrying out of the strategy becomes explicit. "Strategies do not need to be deliberate, they can also emerge, more or less, from the actions undertaken". Mintzberg calls them "emerging strategies", these strategies which appear without any clear intention, or in spite of these intentions, and which are not supported by intellectual knowledge, based on facts and abstract figures, but on an intimate understanding of the company and its environment, rich in details and in colour, resembling more the knowledge the potter can have of his clay.

Far from being a means of creating a strategy, strategic planification only makes it possible to give a form to the implications of a strategy which has already been created, in order to test it or to justify it. Most of the literature consecrated to strategic management concentrates on this last aspect, the formal evaluation of the possible alternatives.

Herbert Simon, intuition is explained by unconscious mechanisms so identical to conscious, rational mechanisms of analysis and of deduction that a large number of these mechanisms can be simulated by a computer.

This viewpoint totally agrees with the cognitivist postulate of unconscious mental processes defined as computations made on symbolic representations. As the recognition of a familiar schema whose characteristic traits have been analysed and stocked in memory, intuition is finally nothing more than "an analysis frozen into habit".

This conception of intuition is like that of psychologists who, like Eric Berne, agree to consider intuition as an unconscious inference coming from subliminal perceptions. From very subtle signs observed subconsciously, such as imperceptible contractions of the muscles around the mouth or around the eyes of the patient, the psychologist infers his personality in a very precise manner. Berne remarks that the unconscious character of this mechanism of observation and of deduction, where only the result appears in consciousness does not affect its effectiveness.

To explain intuition, which he identifies as expert know-how, Hubert Dreyfus postulates, as does Simon, a mechanism of unconscious recognition. But he sees this mechanism as "arational", that is not accompanied by a process of analytic decomposition and recombination.

The unconscious recognition of the similarity between the current situation and a formerly lived situation takes place in a global manner: the former situation is recorded as an image, not decomposed into separate traits. This is how you would explain a chess game, a medical diagnostic, the evaluation of the personnel recruiter....

However, all of these explanations reduce intuition to a deductive or comparative process, and the content of intuition to something already known. None of them enables us to understand the resolution of complex problems, the creation of new ideas, for which no known precedent exists.

In fact the inferential aspect of decision-making which is supported by facts and rules corresponds rather to the knowledge of a novice; to sum up, it expresses an incompetence. Neither does the recognition of a situation enable us to explain a really creative decision. It is really surprising that so few studies have been devoted to the non-analytic, noninferential, non-comparative aspect of decision-making, to the way in which the understanding of a problem, the diagnostic, the new idea just spurts out.

Then, what is the subject's experience, what happens for him ? It is true that the intuitive experience seems to be a very personal and intimate pre-thought-out experience. This know-how, "remarkably efficient, although it does not know itself"—as Piaget says-, entails a character of immediacy which renders it nearly unspecifiable. We know the difficulties encountered by cogniticians to draw out knowledge from experts. Willliam James, distinguishing "knowledge about" from "knowledge of acquaintance" qualifies the latter as "dumb". As for Michel Polanyi, he insists on the difficult-to-transmit nature of this knowledge, which he calls "tacit": "An art which cannot be specified in detail cannot be transmitted by prescription, since no prescription for it exists. It can be passed on only by example from master to apprentice".

SKILLS AND TECHNIQUES OF DECISION-MAKING

We use our decision-making skills to solve problems by selecting one course of action from several possible alternatives. Decision-making skills are also a key component of time management skills. Decision-making can be hard. Almost any decision involves some conflicts or dissatisfaction.

The difficult part is to pick one solution where the positive outcome can outweigh possible losses. Avoiding decisions often seems easier. Yet, making your own decisions and accepting the consequences is the only way to stay in control of your time, your success, and your life. If you want to learn more on how to make a decision, here are some decision-making tips to get you started.

A significant part of decision-making skills is in knowing and practising good decision-making techniques. One of the most practical decision-making techniques can be summarised in those simple decision-making steps:

1. Identify the purpose of your decision. What is exactly the problem to be solved? Why it should be solved?
2. Gather information. What factors does the problem involve?

3. Identify the principles to judge the alternatives. What standards and judgement criteria should the solution meet?
4. Brainstorm and list different possible choices. Generate ideas for possible solutions.
5. Evaluate each choice in terms of its consequences. Use your standards and judgement criteria to determine the cons and pros of each alternative.
6. Determine the best alternative. This is much easier after you go through the above preparation steps.
7. Put the decision into action. Transform your decision into specific plan of action steps. Execute your plan.
8. Evaluate the outcome of your decision and action steps. What lessons can be learnt? This is an important step for further development of your decision-making skills and judgement.

7

MAKING SERIOUS DECISION

Enlightenment is man's emergence from his self-imposed immaturity. Immaturity is the inability to use one's understanding without guidance from another. This immaturity is self-imposed when its cause lies not in the lack of understanding, but in the lack of resolve and courage to use it without guidance from another. Have courage to use your own understanding! Enlightenment means taking full responsibility for your life.

The total effect of the culture and industry is one of anti-enlightenment that is the progressive technical domination of nature, becomes mass deception and is turned into a means for fettering consciousness. It impedes the development of autonomous, independent individuals who judge and decide consciously for themselves.

A free person is the one who know and recognises his/her feasible region e.g., set by his/her society. The slave is not aware of such limits. A free person is wise to recognise what is under his/her control and what is not, and has the ability to accept the first and extend the second one. You may have heard that "If there is a will, then there must be a way". In fact the advice should be in the opposite order, i.e. "If there is a way, then there might be a will". It is right because the feasible region might be empty, and one might ignores one or some constraints, and then being in a big trouble, e.g., willing beyond ones' ability.

The unrealistic expectations of freedom and rights to make your own decisions will destroy a person unless it is recognised that these ideals are privileges and not necessities and therefore they are accompanied by responsibilities. Fear is not in the habit of speaking the truth; when perfect sincerity is expected, perfect freedom must be allowed. Nor does anyone who is apt to get angry when hearing the truth should wonder why he does not hear it.

Mind is what your brain does consciously. Our minds perform a series of information processing in order to form strategies needed to live our daily lives. This process is known as decision-making. However, aside from making decisions, because of many kinds of uncertainties we also face a problem called decidophobia, which is the fear of making the wrong decisions combined with nervous agitation. Moreover, fear of judgement by others is a sure path to unhappiness which is a state of mind.

Decisions are at the heart of success, and at times there are critical moments when they can be difficult, perplexing, and nerve racking. Help and guidance for making efficient and effective decisions by putting to use a well-structured approach and well-focused process known as the modelling or paradigm process. The word paradigm comes from the Greek word paradeigma, meaning "model" or "pattern." A model represents a way of looking at the world, a shared set of assumptions that enable us to understand or predict behaviour. Models have a powerful influence on individuals and on society because our view of the world is determined by our set of assumptions about it. To put it another way, our vision is often affected by what we believe about the world; our beliefs often determine the information that we "see."

Decision-making is about facing a question, such as, "To be or not to be?", i.e., to be the one you want to be or not to be? That is a decision. Humanity has always lived in the shadow of fears. Yet almost nothing was known about fear until Freud began the study of unusual phobias. A little later, some psychologists suggested that one dread is common to all mankind: the dread of death.

The fear of making serious decisions is a new kind of fear, called decidophobia, proclaimed by Walter Kaufmann at Princeton University. The fear of making the wrong decisions is well known to any responsible manager. As Eleanor Roosevelt said, "You gain strength, courage, and confidence by every experience in which you really stop to look fear in the face." Wherever you see a successful business, someone once made a courageous decision. There has never yet been a person in the history of mankind who led a life of ease whose name is worth remembering. The difficulty in life is the choice.

The Latin word Decido has two meanings. It can mean to decide and also to fall off. Hence plants are called deciduous if their leaves fall off in the fall. The word fall started as "leaf fall" for autumn in the 15th century. The expression "take the plunge" suggests the relevance of both meanings. Making a wrong decision provokes the fear of falling.

An effective and proven decision process has been developed over the last 70 years and is known as Operations Research/Management Science/Decision Science/Success Science (OR/MS/DS/SS). In the serious decisions that mold the future of your business, freedom becomes tangible; serious decisions are objects of extreme dread. Serious business decisions that ultimately shape, guide, and direct our future are extremely fearful to business managers. These decisions involve norms, standards, and the comparison and choice of goals.

Learning the structured, well-focused approach to the decision-making process lessens decidophobia. The gem of Applied Management Science is that it turns the old adage that "business managers are born, not made" into myth. If one can master management science applications, then no problem is too big nor any decision too overwhelming. The goal of management science experts is to wipe out decidophobia.

The first requisite for success science is the ability to apply your physical and mental energies to one decision problem/opportunity incessantly without growing weary. Just being worried about making serious decisions is like sitting on a rocking chair--it gives you something to do but doesn't get you anywhere. Therefore worrying about making a decision is a waste of time. A decision is something you have the capability of changing. Anything else is a fact of life.

The first principle in making good decision is that you must not fool yourself, and you are the easiest person to fool. Moreover, making a decision and implementing one are two different things. Here is a question for you: Five frogs are sitting on a log. Four decide to jump off. How many are left? A protracted decision is only one part of the process of choosing because it lacks the commitment to implement the decision. There is a big difference between making a decision and implementing it. The measure of success is not whether you have a tough decision to deal with, but whether it's the same decision you had before. Decide like a man of action; implement like a man of thought. It does not take much strength to decide what to do, but it requires great strength to do things.

Unlike deterministic models (risk-free decisions), the outcome of some decisions depends on the second party, as is the case in any advertising campaign strategic decisions in a competitive market. Therefore, one of the characteristics of decision analysis problems is that "good" decision-making does not necessarily bring about good outcomes. "How could I have been so stupid?" former USA President, John F. Kennedy, asked after he approved the Bay of Pigs invasion.

A decision usually involves three steps:

1. A recognition of a need: A dissatisfaction within oneself--a void or need;
2. A decision to change--to fill the void or need;
3. A conscious dedication to implement the decision.

So aside from that, we see that making the correct decisions is not only what we want to do, but includes what we have to do. The fool who repeats again and again: "I am bound, I am bound," remains in bondage. The fear of making the wrong decision is what pushes and guides us to making a decision by utilising a scientific approach. This is what Management Science is all about.

One must distinguish between science facts and science fictions. Science fiction is a form of fiction that was developed in the 20th century and deals principally with the impact of imagined science upon society or individuals. Management Science is a science fact which is evolving, self-correcting and, unlike science fiction, not valid for eternity. Whenever science is distorted, sensationalised or even reduced to a pseudo scientific level, a grave disservice is done to the public's attempt to understand scientific facts.

Each and every business day the manager puts many decision questions to the test. The questions must first be identified as problems or opportunities, verified; scaled into mathematical models for which an answer will abound, and then controlled by updating the solutions because of the dynamic nature of business decisions. Mathematics has been recognised as an autonomous interior constructional activity which, although it can be applied to an exterior world, neither in its origin nor in its methods depends on an exterior world.

The criterion of a good mathematical model is confined to its usefulness in making good strategic decisions. This is the absolute core of Management Science approach to decision-making, which is the science of decision-making. Not all science facts have practical usefulness. For example, Darwin's insight had no practical payoff, but he was a revered figure because he changed the way humans see their place in nature.

It is this approach to decision-making that makes the business successful. But it is important to note that such a process does not come easily. Again, this process is of a three-fold origin that encapsulates doctrines of computer integration, mathematical scaling and modelling and finally re-entering new data transformations that will occur as time ticks onward. This is the complex analysis that will deduct our thinking in this regard.

Management Science can help reduce or eliminate the fear of making wrong decisions by providing help with the decision-making process. In fact, management science's goal is to eliminate decidophobia. This is accomplished through the phased processes of management science that dissects the components of the decision into workable elements and allows one to proceed to the decision-making stage with sound knowledge on which to base one's choice. However, if you choose not to use management science, there are plenty of other ways to avoid making decisions.

In The Histories, written in 450 B.C., Herodotus makes the following statement:

> "If an important decision is to be made [the Persians] discuss the question when they are drunk and the following day the master of the house...submits their decision for reconsideration when they are sober. If they still approve it, it is adopted; if not, it is abandoned. Conversely, any decision they make when they are sober is reconsidered afterwards when they are drunk."

What a strange way to make decisions, you might say. Perhaps it is, but there are even stranger methods of human choice.

MISERY OF INDECISIVENESS POPULAR STRATEGIC METHODS

Recourse to someone or even something else: Examples are astrology (not astronomy which is a science), palm readings, looking up at stars, dialing 1-900 psychic friends, telepathy, telekinesis, the aura, crystals, dreams, colours, Feng Shui, numerology, fortune-tellers, etc. Physiognomy is any judgement about a person's character based on external appearance.

For example, in contrast to astrology, one must accept the fact that success is not due to a fortuitous concourse of stars at our birth, but due to a steady trail of sparks from the grindstones of hard work, determination, good planning, and perseverance. When it comes to the future, there are three kinds of people: those who let it happen, those who make it happen, and those who wonder what happened.

In all these popular avoidance strategies, you are better off taking advice from Kermit the Frog. A New York City detective said, "I've gone into hundreds of fortune-tellers, and have been told thousands of things, but nobody ever told me I was a policewoman getting ready to arrest them." Fortune befriends the bold who make good decisions.

Nobody can give you wiser advice than yourself.

False hopes: Hoping for something to happen over which we have no control over its outcome. For example, hoping your aeroplane lands safely while you are just a passenger and not the pilot of the plane. False hope and fear are two sides of the same coin. We can promise according to our hopes that are under our control only (and have some degree of certainty on its outcome), however, we avoid making decisions according to our fears of the outcomes.

Do not think about it: The decision-makers who are waiting for something to turn up, might start with their shirt sleeves. You can either take action, or you can hang back and hope for a miracle. Miracles are great, but they are so unpredictable. Doing nothing about a problem on hand, will certainly get out of control and devour other elements of your business too. You've got to jump off cliffs all the time and build your wings on the way down.

Do anchoring: Give disproportional weights to some information instead of waiting as long as possible, to have all the information.

Sunk-cost conscious: Repeat the same decision because "you have invested so much in this approach (or your current job) that you cannot abandon it or make another decision (or look for a better position)."

Failure to reflect on the problem: Reflection before action is often resisted by some managers. They often feel that reflection takes too much time, requires too much work, or they do not know much about decision problem/ opportunity. Remember that: A man should always be already booted to take his journey.

Look for confirming-evidence: Seek out the information to support an existing preselection and discount opposing ones. To put what you like against what you dislike is the hanky-panky of the mind.

Pray for a miracle: Whatever we pray for, we pray for a miracle. Every prayer reduces itself to this: "Great God, grant that twice two be not four." A miracle is an event described by those to whom it was told by men who did not see it. As Emerson said, "As men's prayers are a disease of the will, so are their creeds a disease of the intellect."

1. The worse things get,
2. The harder people pray,
3. The worse things get.

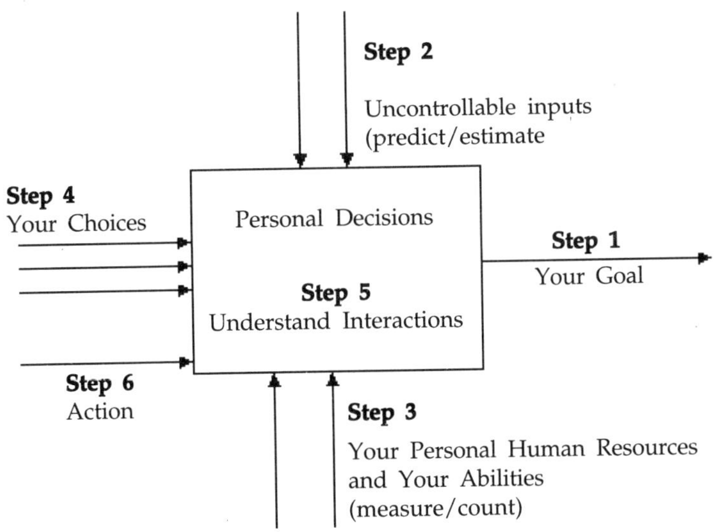

Figure 7.1. Consecutive-focused-thinking as a Mental Modelling Process for Personal Decision-making

Be over-confident: This makes you optimistic and then make high risk decisions. As Henri Poincare said, "Doubt everything or believe everything: these are two equally convenient strategies. With either, we dispense with the need to think for ourselves."

Be too prudent: Be over curious long enough to delay the decision. If you are too careful, you are so occupied in being careful that you are sure to stumble over what you are going to decide. Our doubts are traitors and make us lose the opportunities, by fearing to make our decision. Indecision is debilitating; it feeds upon itself; it is, one might almost say, habit-forming. Not only that, but it is contagious; it transmits itself to others who depend on you.

Misrepresentation: Use argument that "seems" scientific. For example, compute and use the average salary as a typical representative of salary rather than the median.

Pass the buck: Pass off responsibility of making the decision to someone else. Do not make decisions by yourself. Bring in someone to blame if things go wrong. For example, for life's problems some may marry to constantly blame their spouse because it is easier than taking responsibility. Remember that it takes two to tango.

Have second thoughts: Second thoughts have aborted more useful decisions than all the difficult circumstances, overwhelming obstacles, and dangerous detours fate ever could throw at you. Undermining your authenticity by succumbing to someone else's second thoughts is a sinister, subtle, and seductive form of self-abuse.

Succumb to failure: Believe that the choices you will make are predestined and you are bound to fail (one gets used to failure) versus the result of hard work and thought.

Set up a committee: To make decisions, try to set up a committee not necessarily consisting of experts. So if everything goes well, every member is proud of such a decision. But if everything goes wrong, nobody is responsible. Every member would say, "It was not I; it was the committee's decision. You see, we couldn't agree, therefore we voted". Put a face to a faceless group, call it "the committee." A committee is an animal with four back legs.

The committee's members, who are wishing that just to vote in "either/or" fashion are those who are not able to contribute to the decision-making process, therefore shouldn't be trusted with an important decision. A group decision support system could be a technologically advanced version of this strategy. Of course setting up a committee could be done correctly with the proper experts. A committee is a cul-de-sac down which ideas are lured and then quietly strangled. The greatest things are often accomplished by individual people, not by committees.

What does it mean to say that committee might have a responsibility? Committee cannot have a responsibility any more than the business can. The only entities that can have responsibilities are people.

False decentralisation: Decentralisation could take place when an authoritative manager delegates accountability to a new "director of..." for every new decision-making problem, but not delegating any authority.

Failure to define the problem: This certainly lends to a wrong solution. Not knowing the problem, any solution is wrong. If you know the problem then, your solution might be good.

Common Sense-based decisions: If you start making decisions on the basis of conventional wisdom or chatter in the hall, generally speaking, you will make the wrong decision. What is called common sense is almost always uncommon.

Failure to understand the problem: This is caused, among others, by subjectivity, irrational analysis, lateness or procrastination, lack of sensitivity, and lack of focus.

Complexity is confusing to the decision-maker: Simplify and even change the problem to something which you have a strategic solution for (e.g. this is committed by many OR/MS/DS/SS analysts when they change the model to fit their strategic solution algorithm).

Rationalisation to limit the course of actions: This strategy is very popular. Stack the cards to make one alternative clearly right and remove all risk.

Reasoning by analogy: Analogies are not made for proof.

Information: Information gathered is not valid. Decisions are often made first and information sought to support the solution, or much of the information gathered is irrelevant to the decision-making.

False alternative: It attempts to box the decision-maker into a corner from which there is no escape except to accept the alternative. "If you are against abortion, you must work for a law against it." This is an example of false alternative, because you may think that a law against it is even worse.

Decision is only symbolic: One will fight hard for a policy and then be indifferent to its implementation.

The Decision-maker has obligations: Sometimes decision-makers act against integrity to meet some critical personal obligations.

Toe the line: When faced with questions such as "What should I do?", "How should I live?", etc., you may "Toe the line", that is, follow the group, don't disagree and do what others are doing in your profession as men in uniform (i.e., one form) do.

Best of all, decline responsibility: Some shrugged their shoulders as if to shake off whatever chips of responsibility might have lodged there. Stagnate or do nothing is another possible one. Some people do this in belief that the right strategic solution will eventually become obvious. Decline all responsibility, or better still, do nothing; i.e., status quoism. However, "not to decide is to decide". A business manager makes decisions. Whether they are right or wrong, they get made, and they are clear. A weak manager procrastinates and gives false signals, leaving subordinates to charge off in different directions. To avoid criticism do nothing, say nothing, be nothing. The choice not to choose is the choice to remain unconscious and, therefore, to wield power irresponsibly.

Post-decision anxieties: The more highly desirable the alternatives that must be rejected and the faster the decision must be made, the greater are these anxieties (also known as cognitive dissonance). Most people accentuate the positive in their decision and deny or ignore the positive aspect of the rejected alternatives.

Misattribution of causes: Attribute your own success to your skills and hard work and your failures to unavoidable external forces. Do the opposite for other people's success and failure.

Your anxiety is directly proportional to your mental modelling process of reality, for you bring on yourself unlimited fears and unrealistic desires. Decision-making involves a series of steps. The mental modelling process begins with the formation of goals and proceeds to the identification of problems and alternative courses of action. It does not end until well after the decision or choice is actually made and the post decision anxieties have been experienced. Decision-making, however, is one management function that is important at all points in the process of management.

DECISIONMAKING: OVERCOMING SERIOUS INDECISIVENESS

Do not make any serious decisions because you are angry, hurt, depressed, desperate, or frightened. Do not make decisions just to get revenge or to harm someone else. Do not make decision when you are incapable of rational thought. Make decision for the right reasons and when you are calm and thoughtful. Even at these states of mind you must decide whether making any decision is necessary or desirable. Spend some careful thought before acting, so that you will not end up making unnecessary problems.

The following sets of situations for avoiding decision-making are legitimate and appropriate. These conditions include: depression and other mental illness which impairs decision-making functions, coercion, and revelation states. There are situations when you should not make serious decisions. For example, depression is the inability to construct a future. Suppose a person in an executive position within a company has Depression, which is a mental disease, he or she should not be in charge of making serious decisions while being under medical treatment.

Otherwise, it could be costly to the company For example, the well-publicised case of the Norwegian Prime Minister depression situation, he conquered his depression to assume his usual responsibilities after staying out of office for a few weeks. You might have read A Beautiful Mind: The Life of Mathematical Genius and Nobel Laureate John Nash, or seen its movie version, A Beautiful Mind. Richard Nixon claimed that, "I was under medication when I made the decision to burn the tapes."

Coercive decision-making: Coercive persuasions are Mind Control tactics which are part of a Brainwashing practice. They are designed to greatly modify a person's self-concept, perception of reality, and interpersonal relations. When successful, they influence the victim's Thinking Straight ability. Brainwashing is a very intricate process that consists of two stages:

1. One is Conditioning and used for controlling the mind of the victim, e.g., inducing manipulative guilt, covert fear, intimidation, mental and moral confusion, eliciting confessions to uncommitted crimes, and propaganda.
2. The other is Persuasion to cause an inability to think independently, e.g., implanting suggestible impulses into the victim's mind.

Coping with such an inhumane treatment by other people requires first of all that one should never allow the feeling that he/she is a victim but rather a survivor:

1. Victims ask for pity, Survivors look for challenge.
2. Victims worry about who is to blame.
3. Survivors find a way to make a difference.
4. Victims complain; Survivors take action.

The most effective propaganda and indoctrination system is one where its victims do not think they are being propagandised and indoctrinated. We are all familiar with "mild" persuasive techniques used in commercial advertising campaigns to influence consumers' buying behaviour. "They" tell us we'll be healthier, happier, sexier, smarter if only we purchase their products. Many people are unhappy, and neurotic today partly because advertising has caused them to have unrealistic expectations of life, themselves, their jobs due to the fantasy-land products and services that are constantly pushed on them.

Solving a problem by creating a new one: Often, because of deep frustrations in facing a difficult problem, one may unfortunately solve it by creating a bigger problem. This strategy tries to get rid of a present problem with the unfortunate by product of forming a new problem. For example using alcohol instead of facing the difficulties of the problem courageously will only result in the realisation that if alcohol kills germs it also removes personal dignity. In reality, the "happy-hours" are followed by the misery of addiction. Every solution may have a problem.

8

PERSONAL DECISION-MAKING

Many people believe that predetermined destiny rather than their own decisions govern the affairs of their lives. Personal mastery teaches us to choose. Choosing is a courageous act that entails opting for various courses of actions that will define one's destiny. Destiny is not a matter of chance. It is a matter of choice. Striving for goals that do not reflect your values and consequently do not make your life joyful is how we make ourselves unhappy. But if you do not know what you want, then how will you know how to achieve it? Have a very clear picture of what you want out of life and what it will take to get it. There is a popular, classic song in which a raspy female voice exclaims to her independent female audience, "use what you got.....to get what you want."

Be realistic about your abilities. When there is a way, there is a will. The opposite is not true as many people unfortunately believe and have taken as the basis for decisions concerning their personal life. Thinking about strategies to strive after that are beyond your abilities can ruin your life. If a goal is unattainable and you go after it anyway, the consequential failure may cause you pain and diminish your energy (and resources of the organisation). You do best in your profession and your personal life by doing well with respect to your capacity and values rather than trying to do better than another person or organisation. Judge your success by what you had to give up in order to get it. Remember that, if you are attempting the impossible, you will fail; therefore ask what is possible for you.

He knows not his own strength that has not met challenge. When you are facing a decision, then you are sounding-out the depth of your own strengths and the richness of your resources. One is responsible for one's own life. Passivity provides no protection: One must accept responsibility for a decision before one can make any decision.

All religions, arts, philosophy, morality, and sciences are branches of the same tree. All these aspirations have pondered the search for what constitutes a good life. Yet only in the last decades has the study of well-being become a scientific endeavour. The results indicate that the goals and values of personal life are very subjective and mostly cultural. Most people spend a lifetime searching for happiness. They chase idle dreams, addictions, religions, even other people, hoping to fill the emptiness that plagues them. The irony is that the only place they ever needed to search was within. Moreover, once a doctrine, however irrational, has gained power in a society, millions of people will believe in it rather than feel ostracised and isolated.

One must decide for oneself: Leaders and followers face different problems. The leaders have to wonder if the followers will follow them faithfully and the followers wonder if the leader will bring them to the "promised land". In essence, the leaders and the followers are slaves to each other's needs.

There are many factors that contribute to being a good decision-maker, the cardinal ones are:

1. *Self-esteem (not pride):* Self-esteem is a big factor in making good decisions. Some people easily pressured into doing things by others are easily told what to do because they have very low self-esteem. Never feel sorry for yourself — it has a deadly effect on your thinking. Recognise all problems, no matter how difficult, as opportunities for enhancement and/or affirmation of your life, and make the most of these opportunities. Creativity in making good decisions requires having a clear mind.
2. *Courage:* Courage is doing what you are afraid to do. There can be no courage unless you are scared. Courage is to think for yourself. When one has low self-esteem one can be talked into doing almost anything because one depends on others too much for advice. This is all because one may not have strength and courage to listen to his/her own thoughts. There are many ways to escape from your own strategic thinking engagement. For example, have you asked yourself why you read newspapers? Could it be an escape device? As a reporter puts it "Fact that is fact every day is not news; it's truth. We report news, not truth." It may be a shock to most of us that, Thomas Jefferson said, "I do not take a single newspaper, nor read one a month, and I feel myself infinitely the happier for it." You ought to never try to avoid the duty of making up your mind for yourself. If you do not make decisions for yourself, others do it for you: "You're legally allowed to drink now so we figured the best thing for you was a car."

Of all the gifts that a parent can give a child, the gift of learning to make good choices is the most valuable and long lasting. It is the nature, and the advantage, of courageous people that they can take the crucial questions and form a clear set of alternatives. The weak always have to decide between alternatives that are not their own.

It takes education and courage to gain more self-esteem to be positive or confident in decision-making. Listen to yourself and think for yourself. This won't get you into trouble because of someone else. Courage means the act of intelligent risk taking while looking forward into the future. Nothing splendid has ever been achieved except by those who dare, as something inside them was superior to circumstance in making their decisions.

Honesty: Honesty is to be the one you are. Be objective about yourself and others. It is important to identify your weaknesses as well as your strengths. Being honest with yourself is the most important thing you can ever do. When it comes to yourself, you have to be brutally honest.

Love: Love means caring about yourself and other people. It means that you go to sleep at night knowing that your talents and abilities were used in making decisions that, served others. The wonderful thing about love is that it embraces, without binding. To be honest, you must fully accept that at this moment, you can only be what you are. No more, no less; however, with the inevitable passing of each moment of time, you will gradually, but surely change — to become more or less, better or worse, stronger or weaker. Your choice is the direction of change: it is yours alone. The only true competition is the rivalry within your changing self. It is the very basis of a good decision-making.

Hard Decisions: Only you can change your life. No one can make decisions for you when it comes to serious questions, such as, What ought I to do?, What should I believe?, What can I know?, How should I live? What Ralph Waldo Emerson tells us is that the only good answers to such questions are personal and examined ones, rarely those adopted by large groups; conscious, reasoning minds should neither pray to strange Gods, nor encourage the vanities of the self. That alone can set us on the path to freedom.

All the interest of your education should come together to make decisions for yourself. What is the use of education if you cannot face these questions to your own satisfaction? While you are making these decisions, you feel for the time being that your life is your own. Do not envy others, because who envies others does not obtain peace of mind. Everything starts with yourself — with you making up your mind about what you're going to do with your life.

The more amiability and esprit de corps among the members of a policy-making in-group, the greater is the danger that independent critical thinking will be replaced by group think, which is likely to result in irrational and dehumanising actions directed against out groups. Major decisions require courage. We must have courage to bet on our decisions, to take the calculated risk, and to act.

Finally, in personal decision-making there is no one better to talk to than yourself if you really want to get things worked out. No other person has as much information about your problems, and no one knows your skills and capabilities better.

Self-realisation: Maslow's work specifies that individuals have a hierarchy of needs ranging from basic needs for survival and safety to higher-level needs for esteem and self-actualisation as shown in the Fig. 8.1.

Physiological needs: These are primarily biological needs. They include such things as the need for adequate nutrition, shelter, warmth and medical care.

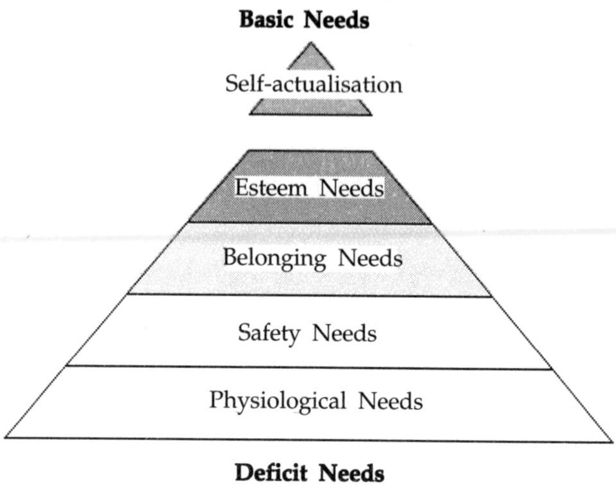

Figure 8.1.

Safety needs: After physiological needs, the second most compelling needs that individuals face are safety and security.

Belongingness and love needs: When physiological and safety needs have been addressed, the next set of needs — those related to belongingness, affection and love — can emerge.

Esteem needs: If the first three needs are fulfilled, the need for esteem may become dominant. This refers both to self-esteem and to the esteem a person gets from others.

Self-actualisation needs: The highest level of needs, those that individuals are able to satisfy when all other more basic needs have been met, is the need for self-actualisation. Self-actualisation is a person's need to be what he/she is. A musician must make music, an artist must paint, a poet must write, if he is to be ultimately at peace with himself.

Popular strategies in avoiding personal decisions: Decisions shape our personal lives, however decision-making can be a stressful, bewildering personal responsibility. Decidophobia is the fear of making your own decisions. The comparison and choice of goals and standards arouses the most intense decidophobia but the only way to ensure stability in the strategic thinking is to engender fear.

In the past few decades, the field of decision-making has concentrated on showing the limitations of decision-makers—that is, that they are not very rational or competent and their thoughts are clouded with a plethora of possibilities, variables and outcomes. In short, there is the lack of a well-focused structured decision-making process.

The following strategies or combination of them enable decidophobes to avoid making their own decisions.

Religion: Religion and the proclamation of what is good and evil is the most popular one. It is through this unity that the decidophobe avoids confrontation. Instead of inviting us to evaluate alternative standards, it gives us norms as well as detailed standards. However, moralising and morals are two entirely different things and are always found in entirely different people.

Every religion too, is a model for questions such as: How should I live, What should I believe? How should I behave? What should I do and so on. In Islam, for example, a man may have more than one wife (officially up to four, at any given time), but he should not drink wine. In Christianity the opposite is allowed. Here you have a choice.

Models are always changing to adapt to reality. For example, Martin Luther, and John Calvin among others, found a need for reformations and modified the Catholic model. The same happened with the Eastern models, such as Buddhism which is the reformed Hinduism. Models, in general, should be able to provide "insights" useful to cope with the decision problem.

In the case of religious models, the question "how should I live?" is not a decision problem. The imperative and authoritative answers to almost all similar decisions are already given. However, there is only one big decision one must make first — "the leap of faith." While the organised religions are life-enhancing for those who need their services, they are not life-affirming.

The source of all religion and metaphysics is the recognition of a higher power, such as a god(s), or "the-thing-in-itself", respectively. Much of what passes for religious faiths, and metaphysics idols (i.e., ideas) amounts to a side bet, covering a vague belief that "there must be something" or that man needs to believe. Philosophy and religion are accustomed in constructing models such as, metaphysics of a higher world, and another-world, in order to despise this world.

The beauty of religious mania is that it has the power to explain everything. Once God (or Satan) is accepted as the first cause of everything which happens in the mortal world, nothing is left to chance. Logic can be happily tossed out the window. Metaphysics are the concepts that empirical investigation is unable to tackle such as the nature of time and gravity, space and the purpose of our beings.

Believing in God, while is sometimes advantageous health-wise, can have the reverse effect: it can predict mortality. A study of 600 older hospital patients, 95 per cent of whom were believers, found that people who felt alienated from God, or who blamed the devil for their illness, had a 19 per cent to 28 per cent increased risk of dying over the following two years.

Drifting: Instead of choosing how to live and what to believe, The drifting person simply follows the "status quo". On the opposite end of the spectrum is the person who has no ties, no code of conduct, or purpose. These types of individuals are afraid of making any decision, no matter how small.

Allegiance to a movement: This strategy identifies the people who are dissatisfied both with traditional life styles and with being adrift, so they join a movement. This is an indication of a person's fear of "standing alone".

Allegiance to a school of thought: This strategy helps to give one an identity. People of this nature share a way of thinking and deal with problems in the same way.

Exegetical thinking: In this strategy one reads in the text, assumes that the text that one reads is right and therefore, treats it as an authority. This enables the exegete to read his own ideas into the text and get them back endowed with authority. The exegetical thinker fears independence and independent thinking.

Manachaeism: For the Manachaeist, the decision is most important and generally makes itself; the choice is loaded. It is when all the odds are stacked, all the good is on one side, all the evil on the other. It ignores all other alternatives.

Moral rationalisation: The idea is that the moral rationalist, through rational thought, can make decisions. However, that moral rationalism may involve an inadequate conception of reason and responsibility. Man —a reasoning rather than a reasonable animal.

Pedantry: This strategy emphasises on a "microscopic distinction". Decidophobia engulfs the pedantic person, as they never get around to considering major decisions and do not look at, or see, the big picture. Action always generates inspiration. Inspiration seldom generates action.

The wave of the future: Although this strategy overlaps with religion, allegiance to a movement or to a school, and to ignore other alternatives and, like other strategies, there is a fear of standing alone and unsupported. Ideals are acceptable because they are "the wave of the future". Idealism increases in direct proportion to one's distance from the decision problem.

Marriage: One of the most popular strategies is that of marriage. This strategy is based on the premise that in marriage, the decisions are left, in most cultures to the husband. However, either spouse can succumb. Decisions are either a consensus of the two or there is a disagreement and one ends up "going along" with the other.

DETERMINATION OF VALUES

Not to arrive at a clear understanding of one's own values is a tragic waste. You have missed the whole point of what life is for. Which one of the following fits your value system? The major value in life is what you get, OR the major value in life is what you become.

Setting a Clear Goal: What is it you want to accomplish? Strangely enough, many decision-makers collect a set of alternatives (say cars to buy or person to marry) and then ask, "Which should I choose?" without thinking first of what their goals are, what overall objective they want to achieve. Next time you find yourself asking, "What should I do? What should I choose?" ask yourself first, "What are my goals?"

Know Your values and preferences: Value refers to how desirable a particular outcome is, the value of the alternative, whether in dollars, satisfaction, or other benefit. However, preference reflects the philosophy and moral hierarchy of the decision-maker. Personal values determine the preferences. Some people prefer excitement to calmness, taking too much risk to a calculable risk, efficiency to esthetics, quality to quantity, and so on.

It is not hard to make good decisions when you know what your values are. However, a question that has inspired many theories conveys the impression that the numerous theories of values and valuation are deeply heterogeneous, some being rational and some irrational, some seeing values as the mere effect of social inculcation, others the effect of emotional factors, as resentment. Moreover some theories attempt to derive values from self-interest, others from the constraints imposed by society on individuals.

Rational choice model: Rational theory deals with one of the major "rational" theories used today to explain norms and values: the so-called "Rational Choice Model". In the expression "Rational Choice Model" the word rational is used in an indigenous fashion, as an equivalent of "instrumentally rational." An action is "rational" in this sense if it can be held as representing objectively a good way of reaching the goal the subject is following. While its supporters see it as a potentially universally valid theory, in other words as the only one actually able to explain indistinctly all human activities, this claim seems ungrounded.

Relativistic vs. naturalistic theories: The interest and limits of these theory deal with the question of which values should be considered as the emanation of singular cultures and, for this reason, vary from one culture to another. These models are dominant today because they defend a relativistic view of values and treat the perception people have of the reasons as to why they endorse such and such values as illusory. Some opponents of the relativistic theories have instead a naturalistic theory of values. It takes its inspiration from sociobiology.

Axiological rationality: Axiological rationality was studies by Weber in distinction between axiological rationality and instrumental rationality.

The instrumental rationality deals with the relations between means and ends, the notion of axiological rationality introduces the idea of a non-consequential type of rationality. This idea can be presented as a sequential type of rationality rather axiological rationality. The explanation of axiological feelings is concerned with the cases where social actors act in conformity with their values.

Cognitivist model: Cognitivist model is a generalisation of the Rational Choice Model which starts from the idea that the notion of rationality has two very different meanings: The sense of the concept in economics, and the philosophy of science. It implies that some irrational people can be interpreted rationally, provided the notion of rationality is adequately defined. It is also concerned with the development of the "judicatory" or "cognitivist" theory of rationality.

The cognitivist model is also applied to the analysis of the feelings of justice in an attempt to apply the judicatory theory of values to a well-circumscribed field: the feelings of justice.

Philosophers, such as Rawls, propose implicitly a theory as to what people mean when they perceive a distribution of goods as fair or unfair. They are in some circumstances Kantian (that is, they tend to follow principles of universal value), while they are rather in other circumstances utilitarian. Concepts such as "local justice" or "bounded justice" are concerned with building a bridge between reality and theory on the feelings of justice.

Fig. 8.2. depicts the dynamic nature of the needs and values in personal decision-making process:

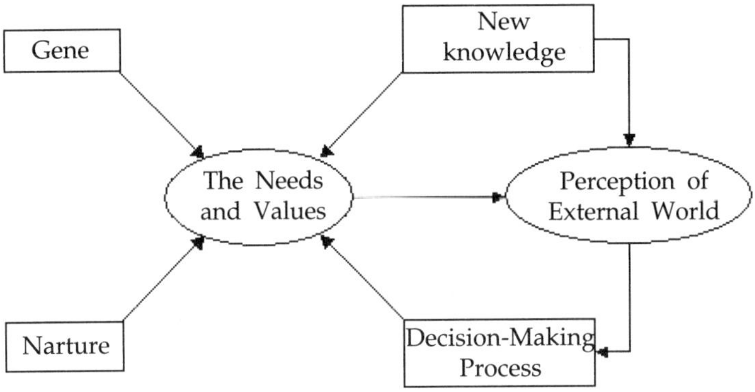

Figure 8.2. Dynamic Nature of Needs and Values in the Personal Decision-making

The above figure represents the needs and values causal connections in both space and time, by bring isolated facts from two primary and secondary sources together and help us construct a coherent understanding of the external world. This conditional knowledge is acquired from experience or learned and tie a flexible and highly interrelated network of links along which reasoning is possible and which can be applied to different decision-making situations.

With respect to decision-making, instead of saying that man is the creature of circumstance, it would be more accurate to say that man is the architect of circumstance. It is character, which builds an existence out of circumstance. From the same materials one man builds palaces, another hotels; one warehouses, another villas; bricks and mortar are mortar and bricks until the architect can make them something else.

The ultimate goal of human decisions is always the satisfaction of the acting man's desire, which is almost always "growth". There is no standard of greater or lesser satisfaction other than individual judgements of "values" and determination of "ranks" among those values. The values and their ranks are different for various people and for the same people at various times.

A potential problem is deciding the importance of the things you think about most of the time. The solution to this problem is to come-up with some criteria in evaluating the degree of the values you hold dear for achieving living well. We have to give meanings to our individual life, otherwise our lives are blank and senseless.

The first task in making private and personal decisions is to find out what the "values" are, for what? The answer is for the enhancement and affirmation of your life. Moreover, one must decide about the "ranks" among these values and their relation to the other values. The following is an ordered three-category model:

— *Group A:* This most important group includes all the things that you can do for yourself and no one else can do for you. Examples include "a good night's sleep", learning to think for yourself, and your health. As a Spanish proverb says, "A man too busy to take care of his health is like a mechanic too busy to take care of his tools." You know it well that "Your health is your wealth." Remember that you will be as much value to others as you have been to yourself.

— *Group B:* The things which are yours and could not have been anybody else's. For example, your child belongs in this group.

— *Group C:* All other things. Such as your house, your job, etc.

9

APPROACHES TO ETHICAL DECISION-MAKING

Ethics refers to standards of behaviour that tell us how human beings ought to act in the many situations in which they find themselves-as friends, parents, children, citizens, businesspeople, teachers, professionals, and so on.

It is helpful to identify what ethics is not:

1. *Ethics is not the same as feelings*: Feelings provide important information for the ethical choices. Some people have highly developed habits that make them feel bad when they do something wrong, but many people feel good even though they are doing something wrong. And often our feelings will tell us it is uncomfortable to do the right thing if it is hard.
2. *Ethics is not religion*: Many people are not religious, but ethics applies to everyone. Most religions do advocate high ethical standards but sometimes do not address all the types of problems we face.
3. *Ethics is not following the law*: A good system of law does incorporate many ethical standards, but law can deviate from what is ethical. Law can become ethically corrupt, as some totalitarian regimes have

made it. Law can be a function of power alone and designed to serve the interests of narrow groups. Law may have a difficult time designing or enforcing standards in some important areas, and may be slow to address new problems.

4. *Ethics is not following culturally accepted norms*: Some cultures are quite ethical, but others become corrupt -or blind to certain ethical concerns (as the United States was to slavery before the Civil War). "When in Rome, do as the Romans do" is not a satisfactory ethical standard.

5. *Ethics is not science*: Social and natural science can provide important data to help us make better ethical choices. But science alone does not tell us what we ought to do. Science may provide an explanation for what humans are like. But ethics provides reasons for how humans ought to act. And just because something is scientifically or technologically possible, it may not be ethical to do it.

Making good ethical decisions requires a trained sensitivity to ethical issues and a practiced method for exploring the ethical aspects of a decision and weighing the considerations that should impact the choice of a course of action. Having a method for ethical decision-making is absolutely essential. When practiced regularly, the method becomes so familiar that we work through it automatically without consulting the specific steps.

The more novel and difficult the ethical choice we face, the more we need to rely on discussion and dialogue with others about the dilemma. Only by careful exploration of the problem, aided by the insights and different perspectives of others, can we make good ethical choices in such situations.

ETHICS AND MORALITY

Morality is a system of rules that modifies our behaviour in social situations. It's about the doing of good instead of harm, and it sets some standard of virtuous conduct. Evaluating the difference of doing well versus harm and to what extent is subjective but this does not preclude us from attempting to find common ground. Often one identifies five principles in common morality:

1. *Autonomy:* This relates to the question of exploitation of others and impacting their freedoms. Almost every decision has impacts on multiple persons and taking these impacts into not only consideration but engraining them in the process is not easy but necessary.
2. *Non-malfeasance:* Will we be creating harm towards others? In government almost every regulation benefits one group while hurting another. The same holds true in the majority of business decisions – action creates a situation that by its very nature benefits some while does not for others.
3. *Beneficence:* Can this create good? A generic statement but worth considering and in essence all one needs to ask is can we solve the identified problem in a way that creates the most good.
4. *Justice:* Is the process fair itself and is the resulting implementation fair. Essentially both the means and the end must be considered. The world is not equal nor should it be as all people are not created equal and what a boring place it would be if we were. There is all the difference in the world between treating people equally and attempting to make them equal.
5. *Fidelity:* Does this follow the professional, corporate or governance roles as defined. Often this involves

looking at the bigger picture and understanding the spirit of your role beyond straightforward results.

As you will have no doubt noticed these definitions are far from concrete or straightforward principles to apply. Every person potentially will have different perspectives or degrees of agreement in each case. However, great strides will have been made if each person is evaluating their concept of ethics. One of the greatest dangers in this field is people ignoring the concept due to the ambiguity.

Impact on Decision-making

There are six key stages identified in the decision-making process which include in order:

1. *Identification of the problem:* Although this is the first stage this may be where morality can have the greatest impact. This is often the most difficult stage for the researcher and if it is not completed properly the results will be unsatisfactory regardless of the quality (or morality) of the work that follows. The framework that is built here constrains or sets the scope of the project. From an ethical perspective the first question of importance may be – is this really a problem at all? More times than not the focus of problems relates to the reduction of costs or increase in revenue. At this point the problem needs to be resolved by a choice of means, which many find unfavourable. Some proponents of ethical decision-making challenge decision-makers to evaluate whether the perceived problem truly is a problem. It sounds simple but in reality the process of considering all the potential alternatives, including do nothing, is not common. Business leaders are engrained with the belief that flexibility, change and adaptation are the answers.

2. *What is the goal:* The dilemma here is whether the goal is to solve the problem in an ethical manner or simply determine the most ethical goal. The conflict here is do you select a goal and then try to implement it in an effective matter later or do you choose your goals based on ethics. In a perfect world it would be optimal to choose a goal with ethics in mind, but in reality the maximised business goal is optimised by considering ethics in only a very general sense at this stage. Eliminate the few obvious options that are unlikely to have any ethical implementation and proceed forward.
3. *Possible actions:* Pending your theory on determining the goal will have a huge influence on the types of actions that make sense. Actions are primarily determined by the goal you wish to achieve. Nevertheless ethics should influence the actions you are willing to take within the scope of your goal.
4. *Predict outcome:* This may be the one stage in which ethics requires no change. Quantitative techniques are straightforward and merely calculate the results based on your inputs. The age-old computer theory of 'garbage in – garbage' out applies.
5. *Pick the best alternative:* Is the best alternative simply the predicted outcome which maximises goals or does it merely provide empirical results for comparison (with which you can rid the outliers). Formulate the choice as a maxim for all similar cases is a concept those in favour of ethics will promote. This is a recurring theme which involves looking outside any particular situation and seeing the forest for the trees.
6. *Implement decision:* In many cases this is an area where morality already plays a significant role in

current business practice. Unions and significant regulations exist to ensure change is 'ethical'. However, real influence is found long before implementation. At this point you are just trying to minimise or trivialise perceived problems in the selected decision. Nonetheless for that reason it is important that decision-makers consider the impacts of implementation. Hopefully if no satisfactory implementation can be found than the problem will be revisited rather than selecting the best of a group of bad choices, which is widespread.

An Application

Medical and Health-Care decision-making have been around since the time when Hippocrates developed his famous hippocritical oath for healers. This ancient philosopher wrote an oath that addressed the professional and ethical issues faced by physicians in their pursuit of healing individuals. The age-old problem has been how does a human being make such an important decision without any rhyme or reason?

Throughout time mistakes have led to the death of sick people. These mistakes have been made because of bad Medical and Health-Care decisions. Most of the major medical schools educate their students through a series of didactic methods and practical experience. The instructors have always taught using research and examples, yet there has not been a formalised mathematical approach to making Medical and Health-Care decisions due to the high subjectivity to these kinds of decisions. Scientific research can eliminate definitively wrong decisions. However, with the fact that humans are the most complex entities in the world, decisions can not be a "one-size-fits-all".

Lobby groups and labour unions are very interesting examples that potentially compromise ethics even though in many circumstances they have good intentions. By promoting the needs of a few over those of many can be considered unethical. This relates to David Ricardo's comparative advantage of the nation. These groups also have a direct negative impact on people who are not a part of these groups. Yet it seems strange at first glance that promoting the interests of workers could in fact be immoral. The problems lies in the fact that the benefits do not extend to all workers despite the fact that decades ago these strides did in fact help all. However, now legislation exists to cover the most basic protections. One must also consider the fact that we will never know what market corrections may have remedied these issues on its own.

For a decision-maker the impact of lobby groups and labour unions represent an area of misconduct on either side. Resources and funds that could be used in production are now allocated to tasks, which do not further a country's growth. Some will argue that if business leaders had used ethical decision-making then the need for unions would not have been required. You could also argue that getting involved in busting a union is making the ethical decision to improve the economy of the nation. What can be learned from this example? Other than the fact that ethics is not straightforward and that every situation is subjective this leads to the reality that Government has a role to ensure the few common standards are legislated. Beyond that the ultimate guide for a decision lies in the individuals hands.

The morally best course of action in any situation takes matters of economic and technical appropriateness into account. Good process and analysis is not a barrier to morality. The key starts at the first stages of the decision process with problem identification and involves trying to ensure that one looks at the bigger picture and truly understanding what the goals are.

As stated earlier government in USA, plays a role to ensure basic protections are available to the entire population. For a business you have to expect people to be true to themselves. By the nature humans are self-interested and it's a corporation's responsibility to align the self-interest of its employees in the right direction. Corporate culture helps define this direction and can create an environment of ethical decisions.

Once the company culture is entrenched it is then necessary to hire the right people. Individuals make decisions and therefore employees will determine whether ethics are executed or become a problem. Once you have hired the right people it is necessary to have communication throughout the organisation.

Dialogue which includes the exploration of new meaning through discourse will facilitate ethical decisions. This gives the individual decision-maker multiple inputs and a better grasp of the big picture. Finally organisations must be extremely careful to monitor potential situations of conflict of interest.

In this environment individuals will identify the problems, set goals and make decisions within the standard framework, which are both successful and ethical. The decision-making process outlined earlier does not need to be modified but rather an organisation needs to hire ethical people and provide them with an ethical environment.

Effective decision-making and ethics are not mutually exclusive. In fact the utilisation of an analytical decision-making process will often flush out immoral decisions based on merit without any specific intent to do so.

HUMAN SIDE OF DECISION-MAKING

People do most effectively when they understand how their activities relate to the big picture. It gives meaning, purpose and relevance to what they do. For example, long range corporate planning and corporate financial structuring do not directly involve second line managers.

In large organisations a decision-maker becomes valuable only as he recognises the relation of his/her decision to that of all other decision-makers within the organisation because he/she may make more or less, or little difference to the organisation, or may even be replaced. However, in small businesses the decision-maker can make, break, or prove to be very difficult to replace. The following are some practical and useful aphorisms for your strategic thinking while you are practicing applied side of decision science:

— Your company should be run and operated as you would expect it to be if you were the customer.

— Once you've developed a customer base, you have the most cost-effective and direct access to the single best source of future business.

— You don't have to blow out the other person's light in order to let your own shine.

— Components of the game: players, added values, rules, tactics, and scope.

— A player's product is complimentary to yours if customers value your product more when they have the other player's product than when they have your product alone.

— A player is your competitor if customers value your product less when they have the other player's product than when they have your product alone.

— A player's product is complimentary to yours if it's more attractive for a supplier to provide resources to you when it's also supplying the other player than when it's supplying to you alone.

— A player is your competitor if it's less attractive for a supplier to provide resources to you when it's also supplying the other player than when it's supplying to you alone.

Writing a good planning will help your business to grow, both organically and through outside funding, and it is essential to have in order to secure financing, ranging from a small business administration loan to venture capital funding. If, instead of futilely fighting, threatened booksellers looked through the other end of the telescope, they might see that what they perceive as competition might actually be a complement. "Together, we can create an appetite that feeds the industry. If all of us—booksellers, publishers, distributors, and authors—do a good job of selling, more people will buy more books. And if we all work together towards the goal, we and the customers (the readers), will be that much happier."

To prosper soundly in business, you must satisfy not only your customers, but you must lay yourself out to satisfy also the men who make your product and the men who sell it. This is in accordance with the implication of the "divisions of labour" in Adam Smith economics.

The ability to see the situation as the other person sees it, as difficult as that may be, is one of the most important skills a negotiator can possess. It is not enough to know that they see things differently. If you want to influence them, you also need to understand empathetically the power of their point of view and to feel the emotional force with which they believe it. It is not enough to study them like beetles under a microscope; you need to know what it feels like to be a beetle. To accomplish this task, you should be prepared to withhold judgement, as you "try on" their views. They may believe that their views are "right" as strongly as you believe that your views are right. You may see the glass as half full of cold water. Your spouse may see a dirty, half-empty glass about to cause a ring on the mahogany finish. A tenet of Western culture is that there is no pleasure without a price. Basically, there is no free lunch.

There are better uses of your time. When you win the business, you lose money. The incumbent can retaliate. Your existing customers will want a better deal. New customers will use the low price as a benchmark. Competitors will also use the low price as a benchmark. It doesn't help to give your customers' competitors a better-cost position. Don't destroy your competitors' glass houses. However, those who live in glass houses should really do nothing at all! If you don't have a really tough competitor, you ought to invent one since competition is a way of life. Get into bed with the customer.

Say thank you with kindness, not cash. Save the best thank you for your best customers. Say thank you in a way that builds your business. Don't say thank you too quickly, or too slowly. Say that you're going to say thank you. Recognise that you may have to compete for loyalty. Allow your competitors to have loyal customers too. Don't forget to say thank you even if you have a monopoly. Say thank you to your suppliers, as well as to your customers.

Females follow a simple rule—look at all the males, and go for the one with the longest tail. Any female who departed from this rule was penalised, even if the tails had become so long that they actually encumbered males possessing them. This was because any female who did not produce long-tailed sons had little chance of producing a son that would be regarded as attractive. Like a fashion in women's clothes, or in American car design, the trend towards longer tails took off and gathered its own momentum.

Someone suggested that the tails of birds of paradise and peacocks (that have always seemed paradoxical because they appear to be handicaps to their possessors), evolved precisely because they are handicaps. A male bird with a long and cumbersome tail is showing to females that he is such a strong male that he can survive in spite of his tail.

For some products, it is samples. For other products, a limited-time or limited-capacity trial version works well. For still others, it is a public workshop that provides a service. A "starter" product or service lets customers try your lower-end offerings on decision-making in purchasing your high-end, more expensive and complex products.

Even when they are proven wrong, forecasters see it as important to maintain consensus in retrospect. For example, banks maintain as an article of faith that the depth of the last recession and the magnitude of the property market collapse could not have been predicted. If it could have been, those responsible for the lending excesses of the 1980s would be guilty of gross negligence rather than being viewed as helpless victims of events. It is often more important to be wrong for the right reasons than to be correct.

In the unsuccessful pursuit of profits, we have made our pricing so complex that the customers neither understand it nor think it is fair. By moving to a new approach, which emphasises simplicity, equity, and value, we hope to regain the good will of the customers. This is what Value Pricing should be about.

Games to Win Your Arguments

Some games people play in trying to win their arguments are given below:

1. Carry your opponent's proposition beyond its natural limits; exaggerate it; the more general your opponent's statement becomes, the more objections you can find against it. The more restricted and narrow your own propositions remain, the easier they are to defend.
2. Use different meanings of your opponent's words to refute his argument. *Example*: Person A says, "You do not understand the mysteries of Kant's philosophy." Person B replies, "Oh, if it's mysteries you're talking about, I'll have nothing to do with them."
3. Ignore your opponent's proposition, which was intended to refer to some particular thing. Rather, understand it in some quite different sense, and then refute it. Attack something different than what was asserted.
4. Hide your conclusion from your opponent until the end. Mingle your premises here and there in your talk. Get your opponent to agree to them in no definite order. By this circuitous route you conceal your goal until you have reached all the admissions necessary to reach your goal.
5. Use your opponent's beliefs against him. If your opponent refuses to accept your premises, use his own premises to your advantage.
6. Confuse the issue by changing your opponent's words or what he or she seeks to prove. *Example*: Call something by a different name: "good repute" instead of "honour," "virtue" instead of "virginity," "red-blooded" instead of "vertebrates."
7. State your proposition and show the truth of it by asking the opponent many questions. By asking many wide-reaching questions at once, you may hide what you want to get admitted. Then you

quickly propound the argument resulting from the opponent's admissions.

8. Make your opponent angry. An angry person is less capable of using judgement or perceiving where his or her advantage lies.
9. Use your opponent's answers to your questions to reach different or even opposite conclusions.
10. If your opponent answers all your questions negatively and refuses to grant you any points, ask him or her to concede the opposite of your premises. This may confuse the opponent as to which point you actually seek him to concede.
11. If the opponent grants you the truth of some of your premises, refrain from asking him or her to agree to your conclusion. Later, introduce your conclusion as a settled and admitted fact. Your opponent and others in attendance may come to believe that your conclusion was admitted.
12. If the argument turns upon general ideas with no particular names, you must use language or a metaphor that is favourable to your proposition. *Example*: What an impartial person would call "public worship" or a "system of religion" is described by an adherent as "piety" or "godliness" and by an opponent as "bigotry" or "superstition." In other words, inset what you intend to prove into the definition of the idea.
13. To make your opponent accept a proposition, you must give him an opposite, counter-proposition as well. If the contrast is glaring, the opponent will accept your proposition to avoid being paradoxical. *Example*: If you want him to admit that a boy must do everything that his father tells him to do, ask him, "whether in all things we must obey or disobey our parents." Or, if a thing is said to occur

"often," ask whether you are to understand "often" to mean few or many times, the opponent will say "many." It is as though you were to put gray next to black and call it white, or gray next to white and call it black.

14. Try to bluff your opponent. If he or she has answered several of your questions without the answers turning out in favour of your conclusion, advance your conclusion triumphantly, even if it does not follow. If your opponent is shy or stupid, and you yourself possess a great deal of impudence and a good voice, the technique may succeed.
15. If you wish to advance a proposition that is difficult to prove, put it aside for the moment. Instead, submit for your opponent's acceptance or rejection some true proposition, as though you wished to draw your proof from it. Should the opponent reject it because he suspects a trick, you can obtain your triumph by showing how absurd the opponent is to reject an obviously true proposition. Should the opponent accept it, you now have reason on your side for the moment. You can either try to prove your original proposition, as in #14, or maintain that your original proposition is proved by what your opponent accepted. For this an extreme degree of impudence is required, but experience shows cases of it succeeding.
16. When your opponent puts forth a proposition, find it inconsistent with his or her other statements, beliefs, actions or lack of action. *Example*: Should your opponent defend suicide, you may at once exclaim, "Why don't you hang yourself?" Should the opponent maintain that his city is an unpleasant place to live, you may say, "Why don't you leave on the first plane?"

17. If your opponent presses you with a counter-proof, you will often be able to save yourself by advancing some subtle distinction. Try to find a second meaning or an ambiguous sense for your opponent's idea.
18. If your opponent has taken up a line of argument that will end in your defeat, you must not allow him to carry it to its conclusion. Interrupt the dispute, break it off altogether, or lead the opponent to a different subject.
19. Should your opponent expressly challenge you to produce any objection to some definite point in his argument, and you have nothing to say, try to make the argument less specific. *Example*: If you are asked why a particular hypothesis cannot be accepted, you may speak of the fallibility of human knowledge, and give various illustrations of it.
20. If your opponent has admitted to all or most of your premises, do not ask him or her directly to accept your conclusion. Rather, draw the conclusion yourself as if it too had been admitted.
21. When your opponent uses an argument that is superficial and you see the falsehood, you can refute it by setting forth its superficial character. But it is better to meet the opponent with a counter-argument that is just as superficial, and so dispose of him. For it is with victory that you are concerned, not with truth. *Example*: If the opponent appeals to prejudice or emotion, or attacks you personally, return the attack in the same manner.
22. If your opponent asks you to admit something from which the point in dispute will immediately follow, you must refuse to do so, declaring that it begs the question.

23. Contradiction and contention irritate a person into exaggerating his statements. By contradicting your opponent you may drive him into extending the statement beyond its natural limit. When you then contradict the exaggerated form of it, you look as though you had refuted the original statement. Contrarily, if your opponent tries to extend your own statement further than you intended, redefine your statement's limits and say, "That is what I said, no more."
24. State a false syllogism. Your opponent makes a proposition, and by false inference and distortion of his ideas you force from the proposition other propositions that are not intended and that appear absurd. It then appears that your opponent's proposition gave rise to these inconsistencies, and so it appears to be indirectly refuted.
25. If your opponent is making a generalisation, find an instance to the contrary. Only one valid contradiction is needed to overthrow the opponent's proposition. *Example*: "All ruminants are horned," is a generalisation that may be upset by the single instance of the camel.
26. A brilliant move is to turn the tables and use your opponent's arguments against himself. *Example*: Your opponent declares, "So and so is a child, you must make an allowance for him." You retort, "Just because he is a child, I must correct him; otherwise he will persist in his bad habits."
27. Should your opponent surprise you by becoming particularly angry at an argument, you must urge it with all the more zeal. No only will this make your opponent angry, but it will appear that you have put your finger on the weak side of his case, and your opponent is more open to attack on this point than you expected.

28. When the audience consists of individuals (or a person) who are not experts on a subject, you make an invalid objection to your opponent who seems to be defeated in the eyes of the audience. This strategy is particularly effective if your objection makes your opponent look ridiculous or if the audience laughs. If your opponent must make a long, winded and complicated explanation to correct you, the audience will not be disposed to listen to him.
29. If you find that you are being beaten, you can create a diversion—that is, you can suddenly begin to talk of something else, as though it had a bearing on the matter in dispute. This may be done without presumption that the diversion has some general bearing on the matter.
30. Make an appeal to authority rather than reason. If your opponent respects an authority or an expert, quote that authority to further your case. If needed, quote what the authority said in some other sense or circumstance. Authorities that your opponent fails to understand are those which he generally admires the most. You may also, should it be necessary, not only twist your authorities, but actually falsify them, or quote something that you have entirely invented yourself.
31. If you know that you have no reply to the arguments that your opponent advances, you by a fine stroke of irony declare yourself to be an incompetent judge. *Example*: "What you say passes my poor powers of comprehension; it may well be all very true, but I can't understand it, and I refrain from any expression of opinion on it." In this way you insinuate to the audience, with whom you are in good repute, that what your opponent says is nonsense. This technique may be used only when

you are quite sure that the audience thinks much better of you than your opponent.

32. A quick way of getting rid of an opponent's assertion, or of throwing suspicion on it, is by putting it into some odious category. *Example*: You can say, "That is fascism" or "atheism" or "superstition." In making an objection of this kind you take for granted:
    (*a*) That the assertion or question is identical with, or at least contained in, the category cited; and
    (*b*) The system referred to has been entirely refuted.
33. You admit your opponent's premises but deny the conclusion. *Example*: "That's all very well in theory, but it won't work in practice."
34. When you state a question or an argument, and your opponent gives you no direct answer, or evades it with a counter-question, or tries to change the subject, it is sure sign you have touched a weak spot, sometimes without intending to do so. You have, as it were, reduced your opponent to silence. You must, therefore, urge the point all the more, and not let your opponent evade it, even when you do not know where the weakness that you have hit upon really lies.
35. Instead of working on an opponent's intellect or the rigor of his arguments, work on his motive. If you succeed in making your opponent's opinion—should it prove true—seem distinctly prejudicial to his own interest, he will drop it immediately. *Example*: A clergyman is defending some philosophical dogma. You show him that his proposition contradicts a fundamental doctrine of his church. He will abandon the argument.

the assumption that recognition will be optimally adapted to the structure of the environment.

Rationality behaviour is adaptive rational if it is optimised to an organism's environment, i.e. if it helps to achieve its goals and it is consistent with logical rules. How did the idea of reasoning as a means to attain one's goals come about? Humans have a demonstrated capacity for highly intelligent action in achieving goals and thereby promoting the specie's survival and, for some, prosperity. However, at the same time, they embarrass themselves when they have their reasoning and decision processes tested. So, we appear rational from one angle, and irrational from another.

The term "rational" can be used to mean two fundamentally different things: Personal Rationality and Public Rationality. However, both are goal directed. Difficulties often arise when these two meanings are glossed over or confused.

Personal Rationality

Making a decision in a way that is generally reliable and efficient for achieving one's personal goals effectively. This kind of rationality, is 'Purpose-based Rationality'. It implies that the ends always rationalise the means. This is a version of the Machiavellian rationality, where individuals must overcome their social training and traditional ideas to seek their own way of making decisions. You may remember the song titles: "I Gotta Be Me" or "I Did It My Way."

Rational people make decisions that are best for them. This may be in terms of either psychological satisfaction or material gain. If a person carries out all the steps in the decision process and arrives at the resolution stage by the evaluation of the alternatives and predicting the outcomes, that person is regarded as rational if he/she acts upon the best action selected by the process.

Public Rationality

Making a decision sanctioned by the law which requires evidence. This kind of rationality is 'Process-based Rationality' which means that the means must justify the ends. Within the domain of relevant law, it has to be a responsible and defensible decision.

Unfortunately, there are other isolated rationality types, such as the 'proof by pleasure principle' as opposed to the 'proof by contradiction principle'. However, failure to distinguish between these two distinct types of rationality can lead to empty or misleading judgement about human rationality.

Here is a question for you: The debate on abortion belongs to which of these two categories of rationality? Abortion is a "premeditated decision to murder." Or, as a leading feminist declared, "don't put your law into my body." It's a hard decision to make.

Global Social Decisions

In an increasingly globalise world, it is inevitable that many of the social problems which have so far been seen as national in character will assume a global character. Global social problems are those which cannot be confined within national boundaries and which need both national and international attention if they are to be ameliorated.

Pollution of the atmosphere is a stark example of this process. Global Social Decisions must begin with an understanding of the contested concept of globalisation and exploring the global social policies to the most important global social problems: Environmental

Degradation, International Poverty, Crime, AIDS, Drugs, Family Violence, Racism and Migration.

Knowledge and Information

Thinking of them as similar or synonymous distorts the entire concept of managing intangible assets. When we speak or write, we use language to articulate some of the tactic knowledge in an attempt to pass it on to others, it is called information. Knowledge and information are often confused with each other.

In the information technology industry, they are used as synonyms. Thus, the word information is usually associated with both facts and the communication of facts. Information is in many ways ideal for communicating explicit knowledge. It is fast, independent of the originator, and secure.

All three of these features are of vital importance in the information technology era because the computer is designed to handle information. So it is tempting and seems commonsensical for the sender or speaker to attribute information with some sort of meaning. The trouble is people know more than they are conscious of or can put into words. For example, try to explain in words how to drive a golf ball or serve a tennis ball. These concepts are too complex to express fully in words. Attempts to do so are often ridiculous and almost always incomprehensible.

The receiver of information—not the sender—gives it meaning. Information, as such, is meaningless. Information is perfect for broadcasting articulated knowledge but is unreliable an inefficient for transferring knowledge from person to person. It is best not to write but to talk when we wish to transfer knowledge.

Clearly such a distinction between knowledge and information is critical when discussing the contemporary challenge of knowledge management. It is valuable to further delineate different kinds of knowledge, and, more important, to better understand the appropriate means of transferring knowledge to others.

Kinds of knowledge

One of the basic distinctions is the difference between information and knowledge and second to that is the related distinction between explicit and tacit knowledge. When we record what we know, we are making that knowledge explicit in the form of documents, graphics, or other concrete media, this is converting knowledge to information. Any form of knowledge that is made explicit is no longer knowledge but information. A well-used, but nevertheless important, metaphor uses an iceberg to show the relationship between explicit and tacit knowledge.

Tacit knowledge is knowledge that enters into the production of behaviours and/or the constitution of mental states but is not ordinarily accessible to consciousness and is represented by the submerged portion of the iceberg. The part that is exposed above the water is explicit knowledge. The beauty of this analogy is that both the exposed and the submerged are parts of the same chunk of ice. If all you have explicit knowledge, you can't do anything. Tacit knowledge makes explicit knowledge usable.

The three kinds of intellectual capital then are related to this model, with human capital represented by the submerged portion of the iceberg and structural capital by what is above the water. The management of structural knowledge involves raising the iceberg such that what was once human capital is now available to the organisation in explicit form. Obviously, raising an iceberg is not an easy task and the analogy seems appropriate as the mass of tacit knowledge retained by the people in an organisation will never surface. To better represent the portion of knowledge represented by the iceberg that is just below the surface of the water. Implicit knowledge is knowledge that can be codified but has not yet been made explicit.

Explicit knowledge

An organisation can best capitalise on the exposed explicit knowledge by providing the technology and business processes necessary to make this codified content easily accessible to those who need it within the company and to principal customers and suppliers. A significant portion of the resources and effort around knowledge management involves the design, development, and deployment of effective knowledge repositories and document management systems that organise and catalogue, thus providing easy and rapid access to the massive amounts of explicit material that can be generated by a company.

Unfortunately, many of the existing approaches to management of these explicit knowledge assets resemble the way most of us organise our attics. This problem cab be describe using the metaphor of a small used book store where the books are distributed around the room in the cardboard boxes in which the originally arrived. The process for locating what we are looking for involves an exhaustive search through every one of the boxes since no effort was made to organise the content in any meaningful way.

Implicit knowledge

Assuming there is an adequate system in place for handling the explicit knowledge of an organisation, a second management approach involves capturing implicit knowledge by recording it in a structured way and thus converting it into information. This can involve the straightforward documentation of core business processes, procedures, and best-known methods in document form, but can also be the collection of video recordings from key customer or management presentations and conference addresses.

The development of most forms of training and education programmes involves the process of translating valuable expert knowledge into information. The results can be in the form of classroom, computer-based, or on-line training, or reference material utilising streaming audio, video, or a combination of various media.

Tacit knowledge

By definition, tacit knowledge cannot be codified and remains with the individual who developed it through a combination of formal learning and experience. The means for managing this kind of knowledge are not much different from those for managing human resources in general. Competitive processes need to be designed for the effective selection of knowledgeable hires, as well as the development of all employees, plus effective compensation and benefits programmes to retain the talented and knowledgeable people on whom the organisation depends for innovation and decision-making. Specific focus should be on mentoring and apprenticeship opportunities that are the most effective means for transfer of tacit knowledge.

Knowledge and a culture of learning

The explicit culture can be understood and at one level managed by the physical artifacts or documented mission, vision, values, operating philosophies, and policies of the organisation that lie above the surface of the water. The implied culture is simply the actual culture as experienced by the people in the organisation and can be made explicit through observations of the actions, espoused values, attitudes, and decisions that people make. However, at the root, and the most difficult to expose, are the tacit knowledge, basic assumptions, or mental models held by people that give rise to their felt values and ultimately observable behaviour.

Five elements comprise the core learning message to make it compelling in engaging people's passion. They are: a positive vision of the future; inspiring core values; engaging and inclusive leadership style; emotional intelligence competencies; and leadership courage.

10

ENHANCING YOUR DECISION-MAKING SKILLS

Good decision-making is an essential skill for career success generally, and effective leadership particularly. If you can learn to make timely and well-considered decisions, then you can often lead your team to spectacular and well-deserved success. However, if you make poor decisions, your team risks failure and your time as a leader will, most likely, be brutally short.

Decision-making skills will enhance your ability to view any unclear decisions in a different light. Some of these tips you may know, some you may not. Some are even contrary to popular opinion. At least when you come to implement a decision, having read these tips for decision-making, you can say that you are well informed!

RIGHT THING

Many people want to do the thing right. In fact, it is one of the major reasons for delaying decisions. They want to get it right. Peter Drucker, the management guru, insists that it is much more important to do the right thing. Most people really do know what the right thing is. But because it's difficult, disagreeable or uncomfortable, they choose not to make that decision. They choose something different. The consequence is misery. Only the amount and duration varies.

BEST DECISION

Here's another great barrier in decision-making to help you delay some more: The desire to make the best decision. In truth, there really is no way to know which is the best decision. Every decision will have consequences, so what people end up doing is comparing the consequences. This is all well and good, but it makes for an unclear decision. It doesn't actually get anything done.

It's much more useful to consider whether a particular decision will be effective or not, within the frame you choose. People in critical situations quickly learn this decision-making skill. Gary Klein has studied firefighters and medical personnel, people who make decisions in life or death situations. They just don't have time to weigh up the pros and cons. They are asking themselves about the effectiveness of a particular option. If they think it'll work, they go for it.

If at any point along the line they realise it is not working, they choose a different route that they think will work. Then they do that. They will cycle one option at a time, until they find one that works. They improve their decision-making skills with experience in their area of expertise, so their first option is not random. It is the one most likely to work.

So it's much more useful to be effective and get the job done than to spend endless hours trying to determine the best decision.

Again, this is a great one for delaying making that decision. And, of course, it's a myth that you can be 100 per cent sure with people. Humans are complex, dynamic creatures. Life itself is messy and unpredictable. And the future, well, that's an unknown quantity. Period. Enough said.

Most of the decision-making models and processes available are organised around assessing and understanding the issues at hand. The idea is to build your decision-making skills so that you are not engaged in decision-making without critical thinking, but rather you reason and think your way to making good decisions. Occasionally, it is suggested that you actually use your intuition. But not, however, at the expense of logic and rationality.

To develop your decision-making skills, this concept is one to pay attention to. There is an idea that we actually make the decisions emotionally, and then justify it with reasons and explanations, even excuses! An example would be making a decision to buy something that you cannot really afford, but somehow you find a reason that it would be useful to you.

"The stereo costs more than my budget, but it would look great in my room and the great sound would allow me to work more effectively".

Some of the newer sales training programmes use this as the basis for their sales models. Why? Because it works! They know they can make more money using this particular sales model.

Wouldn't it make sense to know your own emotional signals that let you know how to make good decisions? Not only would you be able to make more effective decisions, but others would not have the power to manipulate you!

It is sometimes thought that by not making a decision, you cannot go wrong. The difficulty here, of course, is that not making a decision is often a very poor decision. And not making a decision may actually be a decision to not take action. A classic example is where all the evidence is that there's a career change needed.

It's usually much more effective and useful to make a decision, act, assess as you go along, and change the decision later if indicated. This is obviously easier if the other tips and decision-making skills mentioned above are in place.

MAKE FASTER DECISIONS

Here are some decision-making tips for you to consider before you even make a decision. By considering these ideas, when it comes time to decide, you will know how to make faster decisions. Some of these ideas may be contrary to popular opinion. But they are used by effective decision-makers. Perhaps if more people adopted these decision-making tips, there would be a major shift in people's understanding of how to make great decisions and how to make faster decisions.

When making your decisions, put yourself first. It's important that you're better off as a result of making the decision. And not just in the result that you get, but more especially, as a person. The decision should allow you to maintain who you are, without compromise. This is the first and most important of these decision-making tips if you want to be yourself and live your own life.

If you consider your family important to you, demonstrate this by creating work-life balance in your decision-making. As above, it's important not to compromise your family either. Whatever decision you make, you and your family should benefit in the short-term and in the long-term. Many people, however, use this as an excuse for continuing as they are. The typical example is to say they are working long hours so that the family can have money. The family, of course, want to be spending time with this person. If you prefer working to spending time with your family, then do just this. And don't compromise yourself or them by pretending anything else.

MAKE YOUR OWN DECISIONS

If you allow others to make decisions for you instead of making your own decisions, then they are running your life. In effect, you're giving them control and you are living the life they think you should have.

Take Responsibility

This is a big one. In order to take responsibility for your own decision-making, it's useful to have a strong sense of self and be comfortable in your own skin.

When you do take responsibility many things become available to you.

1. If things don't go according to plan (as they sometimes don't!) you're never a victim.
2. You immediately consider what you can do differently and you act on it.
3. You are free to make a different decision at any time.
4. You are prepared for the consequences, whatever they are.
5. Other people respect you.
6. It makes it easier for them to take responsibility for their own decisions.

Most people want to know how things will pan out before they make a decision. This is a decision mistake and is usually counterproductive. The world is chaotic, unpredictable, and unexpected things happen. It's much more useful to take things one step at a time. To make a decision, you only need to know what the single next step is that will get you closer to your outcome. Then, having taken this step, you make your next decision.

You will notice that some of these decision-making tips overlap. And to implement some of them, it's easier if you have others in place. An important thing to bear in mind when reading these tips for decision-making, is that the whole process is more than the sum of the parts. It is possible to do the individual pieces and then add them up at the end.

Assess and Update

Having made your decision and started into action, it's important to continually assess what's going on. Is what you're doing getting you to where you want to go? If it's not you may need to make a different decision. It seems obvious and yet it's amazing to notice the number of people who think that once they've made a decision they have to stick to it.

Change your Decision Reluctantly

This may seem like a contradiction to the last one of the decision-making tips. Those who are successful in life are able to make decisions quickly, and are slow to change them. People who are not as successful, are much slower in decision-making and tend to change their mind a lot.

There are lots of decision-making tips to be had from studying successful people because they know how to make faster decisions. They generate outcomes and keep them intact. Once they decide to aim for something they keep moving towards it, regardless of the obstacles that arise. People who fail do so because of the first or second hurdle they give up. They change their mind, make a different decision. Then at the next hurdle they make a different decision again.

So do successful people never change their mind? Of course they do. They make a different decision when the information in the environment shifts radically and indicates that it's appropriate to do so. Then they commit 110 per cent to the new decision.

BIBLIOGRAPHY

Allais M., and O. Hagen, *Cardinalism: A Fundamental Approach*, Kluwer Academic Publishers, 1994.

Asch, S. E., "Studies in Independence and Conformity: A Minority of One Against a Unanimous Majority", *Psychological Monographs, **70**(19)*, 1956.

Barton, H., Brown, D., Cound, J., Marsh, P., & Willey, K., "Does Top Management Add Value to Investment Decisions?", *Long Range Planning, **25**(5)*, 1992, 43-58.

Behling, O. & Eckel, N., Making sense out of intuition, *Academy of Management: The Executive*, February 1991.

Bell, D. E., Raiffa, H., & Tversky, A. (Ed.)., *Decision Making: Descriptive, Normative and Prescriptive Interactions,* Cambridge: Cambridge University Press, 1988.

Berne E., *Games People Play: The Psychology of Human Relationships*, Reissue edition, Ballantine Books, 1996.

Bernstein P., *The Power of Gold: The History of an Obsession*, Wiley & Sons.

Blackwell, L., *Dimensions of intuition in higher education*, Ann Arbor, MI: UMI Dissertation Services, 1987.

Borcherding, K., Larichev, O. i., & Messick, D. M. (Ed.)., *Contemporary Issues in Decision Making,* Amsterdam: North-Holland, 1990.

Boudon R., *The Origin of Values: Sociology and Philosophy of Beliefs*, Transaction Publishers, New Brunswick, N.J., 2001.

Brown, A., *The use of intuition in the decision-making processes of public school superintendents*, Ann Arbor, MI:UMI Dissertation Services, 1990.

Cosier, R. & Aplin, J., "Intuition and decision-making: Some Empirical Evidence", *Psychological Reports*, 1982.

Covey S., *The 7 Habits of Highly Effective People*, Running Press, 2000.

Diener E., and E. Suh, (eds.), *Culture and Subjective Well-Being*, MIT Press, 2000.

Dodwell P., *Brave New Mind: A Thoughtful Inquiry into the Nature and Meaning of Mental Life*, Oxford University Press, 2000.

Eisenhardt, K. M., & Zbaracki, M. J., "Strategic Decision Making", *Strategic Management Journal*, ***13***, 1992, 17-37.

Eisenhardt, K., "Making fast strategic decisions in high-velocityenvironments", *Academy of Management Journal*, 1989.

Emery, M., *Intuition workbook: An expert's guide to unlocking the wisdom of your subconscious mind*, New Jersey: Prentice Hall, 1994.

Facione, P. and Facione, N., *Thinking and Reasoning in Human Decision Making*, 2007.

Feeney D., *Motifs: The Transformative Creation of Self*, Praeger, 2001.

Ferrell O., J. Fraedrich, and L. Ferrell, *Business Ethics: Ethical Decision Making and Cases*, Houghton Mifflin Company; 5th ed., 2001.

Fodor J., *The Mind Doesn't Work That Way: The Scope and Limits of Computational Psychology*, MIT Press, 2000.

Fox, William M., "Effective Group Problem Solving: How to Broaden Participation, Improve Decision Making, and Increase Commitment to Action", San Francisco, CA: Jossey-Bass, 1987.

French S., *Decision Theory: An Introduction to the Mathematics of Rationality*, Halsted Press, 1986.

Freud S., *Civilization and Its Discontents*, J. Strachey (editor), Norton & Co., New York, 1999.

Goleman, D., *Emotional Intelligence: Why It Can Matter More Than IQ for Character, Health and Lifelong Achievement*, New York: Bantam Books, 1995.

Harris T., *I'm Ok - You're Ok: A Practical Guide to Transactional Analysis*, Galahad Books, 1999.

Hechter M., et al., *The Origin of Values*, A. de Gruyter, New York , 1993.

Hermann, N., "The creative brain", *Training and Development Journal*, October, 1981.

Isabel Briggs Myers | Myers, I., *Introduction to Type: A description of the theory and applications of the Myers-Briggs type indicator*, Consulting Psychologists Press, 1962.

Jackendoff R, *Languages of the mind*, Essays on mental representation, The MIT Press, Cambridge, 1993.

James Reason, *Human Error*, Ashgate, 1990.

Janis I., and L. Mann, *Decision Making: A Psychological Analysis of Conflict, Choice and Commitments*, Free Press, 1977.

Jensen, M. C., "Organization Theory and Methodology", *The Accounting Review*, ***58***(2), 1983, 319-339.

Johnson, Luke Timothy, "Decision Making as a Theological Process: The Necessity and Difficulty of Discernment," *Sewanee Theological Review 39,* 1996, 353-61.

Kaufmann W., *From Decidophobia to Autonomy: Without Guilt and Justice*, A Delta Book, 1975.

Keeney R., *Value-Focused Thinking: A Path to Creative Decision Making*, Harvard University Press, 1992.

Klein G. *Sources of Power: How People Make Decisions*, MIT Press, 1999.

Lewin K., *Resolving Social Conflicts: Force Field Theory in Social Science*, American Psychological Association Press, 1997.

Maslow A., D. Stephens, and G. Heil , *Maslow on Management*, Wiley, 1998.

Miller, R. B. and Heiman, S. E. *Strategic Selling* Kogan Page, 1989.

Mullen, J. D., & Roth, B. M., *Decision making: Its logic and practice*, Savage, MD: Rowman & Littlefield, 1991.

Nozick R., *The Nature of Rationality*, Princeton Univ. Press, 1994.

Patz, Alan L., "Strategic Decision Analysis: A General Management Framework", Boston, MA: Little, Brown, 1981.

Pelton, Warren J., "Tough Choices: The Decision-Making Styles of America's Top 50 CEOs", *Homewood*, IL: Dow Jones-Irwin, 1990.

Pennings, J. M. (Ed.)., *Decision Making: An Organizational Behaviour Approach*, New York: Markus Wiener Publishing, 1983.

Pettigrew, M. A., *The Politics of Organizational Decision Making*, London: Tavistock Publications, 1973.

Pinches, G. E., "Myopia, Capital Budgeting and Decision Making", *Financial Management*, ***11***, 1982, 6-19.

Plous, S., *The Psychology of Judgement and Decision Making* New York: McGraw-Hill, 1993.

Polanyi M., *Personal Knowledge*, Towards a Post-Critical Philosophy, The University of Chicago Press, Chicago, 1962

Rasmussen, J., Brehmer, B., & Leplat, J. (Ed.)., *Distributed Decision Making: Cognitive Models for Cooperative Work,* Chicester: John Wiley & Sons, 1991.

Rawls J., A Theory of Justice, Belknap Press, 1999.

Reichley J., *The Values Connection*, Rowman & Littlefield Publishers, 2001.

Reynolds V., and R. Tanner, *The Social Ecology of Religion*, Oxford Univ. Press, 1995.

Rosen M., *On Voluntary Servitude: False Consciousness and the Theory of Ideology,* Harvard University Press, 1996.

Schopenhauer A., *The Art Of Controversy*, Kessinger Publishing, 2004.

Soelberg, P. O., "Unprogrammed Decision Making", *Industrial Management Review*, ***8***, 1967, 19-29.

Steiner C., *Scripts People Live: Transactional Analysis of Life Scripts*, Grove Press, 1990.

Twite G. and M. O'Keeffe, *New Directions in Corporate Strategy*, Allen & Unwin, 2000.

Ullman, D. G., *Making Robust Decisions* Trafford, 2006.

Velasquez M., *Business Ethics: Concepts and Cases*, Prentice Hall; 5 ed., 2001.

Virine, L. and Trumper M., *Project Decisions: The Art and Science*, Management Concepts, Vienna, VA, 2007.

Warren S., and A., *Thompson, Dumped!: A Survival Guide for the Woman Who's Been Left by the Man She Loved*, Harpercollins, 1999.

Webster, F. E.; and Wind, Y., *Organizational Buying Behavior* Prentice-Hall, 1972.

INDEX